THE BALTIC EXCHANGE · LONDON *Entrance Hall, showing Commonwealth Coats of Arms*

THE BALTIC STORY

Baltick Coffee House to Baltic Exchange

1744–1994

OUR WORD OUR BOND

To All and Singular

to whom these Presents shall come, the Honourable Sir George Rothe Bellew Knight Commander of the Royal Victorian Order Garter Principal King of Arms and Sir John Dunamace Heaton-Armstrong Knight Member of the Royal Victorian Order Clarenceux King of Arms Send Greeting

Whereas Richard Dennis Hyde Chairman of **The Baltic Mercantile and Shipping Exchange Limited** in the City of London hath represented unto the most noble Bernard Marmaduke Duke of Norfolk Knight of the most noble Order of the Garter Knight Grand Cross of the Royal Victorian Order Earl Marshal and Hereditary Marshal of England and One of Her Majesty's most Honourable Privy Council that the Baltic Mercantile and Shipping Exchange Limited was duly incorporated on the Fourteenth day of January 1900 under the provisions of the Companies Acts 1862 to 1893 as a Company limited by shares for the purpose of providing facilities for speculating Shipping and Commodity markets That the said Company had its origin in an association of Merchants and Ship captains formed in the Reign of King James the First ...

And Forasmuch as the said Earl Marshal did by Warrant under his hand and Seal bearing date the Sixtieth day of June last authorize and direct Us to grant and assign such Arms and Crest and such Supporters and such Device or Badge accordingly **Know ye therefore** that We the said Garter and Clarenceux in pursuance of His Grace's Warrant and by virtue of the Letters Patent of Our several Offices to each of Us respectively granted do by these Presents grant and assign unto **The Baltic Mercantile and Shipping Exchange Limited** the Arms following that is to say Azure three Bars wavy Argent over all a lighthouse between two Lymphads sails set and pennons flying Or in chief a pair of Wings conjoined Gold and for the Crest On a Wreath Argent and Gules Two Mermen respectant proper supporting a Garb Or Banded Argent and Azure as the same are in the margin hereof more plainly depicted And by the Authority aforesaid We do further grant and assign the following Device or Badge that is to say A Garb Or enfiled with a Mercantile Crown Azure the sails Argent as is here depicted to be borne and used upon Standards or otherwise And by the Authority aforesaid I the said Garter do by these Presents further grant and assign unto **The Baltic Mercantile and Shipping Exchange Limited** the Supporters following that is to say On the dexter side a Sea Lion and on the sinister side a Sea Bear both Or and charged on the shoulder with a Pegasus Azure as the same are also in the margin hereof more plainly depicted the whole to be borne and used for ever hereafter by The Baltic Mercantile and Shipping Exchange Limited on Silver or otherwise according to the Laws of Arms **In Witness** whereof We the said Garter and Clarenceux Kings of Arms have to these Presents subscribed Our names and affixed the Seals of Our several Offices this Tenth day of December in the Sixth year of the Reign of Our Sovereign Lady Elizabeth the Second by the Grace of God of the United Kingdom of Great Britain and Northern Ireland and of Her other Realms and Territories Queen Head of the Commonwealth Defender of the Faith and in the year of Our Lord One thousand nine hundred and fifty-seven.

G. R. Bellew.   Garter

J. D. Heaton-Armstrong   Clarenceux

THE BALTIC STORY

Baltick Coffee House to Baltic Exchange

1744–1994

HUGH BARTY–KING

Quiller Press
London

ENDPAPERS: *Drawings by Geoffrey Fletcher*
FRONTISPIECE: *Arms of the Baltic & Mercantile Shipping Exchange Ltd*

First published 1994 by
Quiller Press Limited
46 Lillie Road
London SW6 1TN
ISBN 1 870948 91 2

Designed by Tim McPhee and produced by Debbie Wayment
at Book Production Consultants, Cambridge, for Quiller Press
Typeset by Cambridge Photosetting Services
Origination by Anglia Graphics, Bedford
Printed and bound by The Bath Press, Avon

Acknowledgement is gratefully made to those who have provided illustrations on the pages
indicated. ABP: p. 155; Richard Alexander: p 56; The Baltic Exchange: frontispiece, pp 28–9,
33, 34, 39, 42–3, 50, 53, 62, 69, 70, 75, 76, 78–9, 84, 89–91, 94, 97 right, 138; A Bevington:
p 48; Bibby Line: p 66; J D D Brown: p 156; J Buckley: pp 93, 96 top, 97 left, 167; J E Duggan:
pp 101, 102, 103; E A Gibson & Co. Ltd: p 141; Geoffrey Fletcher: endpapers, p 51; Furness
Withy & Co. Ltd: p 123; Grain & Feed Trade Association: p 49; J Gregory: p 100; Guildhall
Library: facing p1, pp 16, 17, 18, 41; Alan Harper: pp 77, 85; Harris & Dixon Ltd: pp 5, 135;
Intercargo: p 159; A Louis Jarché: p 60; John Good & Sons Group: p 146; John Sutcliffe & Son
(Holdings) Ltd: p 126; Hugh McCoy: pp 108–9; Moray Firth Maltings PLC: pp 150–1;
Ordnance Survey: pp 14–15; Peter Orme: p 106; P & O Steam Navigation Company: p 118;
Pegasus Ocean Services Ltd: p 130; Port of London Authority Collection: pp 20–1, 36–7;
Publifoto: pp 92, 98; Queensland Sugar Corporation: p 161; Robert Enever Associates: p 52;
Dick Sellenrand: pp 144, 164–5; Simpson, Spence & Young: p 129; R Smith: p 96 bottom;
Stephenson Clarke Shipping Ltd: p 117; Turnbull Scott & Company: p 120; David Watkins,
Stephenson Clarke Shipping Ltd: pp 116–17; Jon Whitbourne: p 148; Wijsmuller Holdings BV:
p 154; Arthur D Wright: p 99.
Illustrations on the following pages are from the publications named. *The Baltic:* pp 59, 64 top,
82, 84, 104, 105, 131; Herbert Fry, *London in 1886* (W H Allen & Company, 1886): p 31;
H Clarkson & Company brochure: pp 140–1; Intercargo Annual Review 1993: p 158; *Progress*
(The Unilever magazine): p 55; *Shipping World:* p 44; Vogt & Maguire brochure: p 142;
The Windsor Magazine: p 40.
Every effort has been made to obtain permission for the reproduction of illustrations in this book;
apologies are offered to anyone whom it has not been possible to contact.

CONTENTS

The Lord Mayor of London 1993/4, Paul Newall.

Over the centuries London, with its great river and shipping expertise, has been the centre of the maritime world. Cargoes from all corners of the globe have been bought and sold by merchants in London and landed at the port. With the changes in world trade patterns and the all-embracing sweep of modern technology, physical shipping in the City is less in evidence. However, London remains the maritime centre of the world.

The brokers who match cargoes and ships, buy and sell vessels and deal in the raw materials that drive the world's industrial engines continue to thrive. That the relatively small City market of The Baltic Exchange, with only 1500 trading members, should generate over £400 million a year in invisible earnings is truly a success story for the City.

This book, to celebrate the anniversary of the founding 250 years ago of a coffee house bearing the "Baltick" name, symbolises the key role that the Exchange plays today at the centre of the world's bulk shipping market.

Paul Newall

AUTHOR'S PREFACE

The history of the Exchange that its board commissioned from me in 1970, which ran to four hundred pages, was intended to mark the 150th anniversary of the creation in 1823 of the body called the Baltic Committee. This was formed, by the subscribers to the Subscription Room above William Melton's Baltick Coffee House in Threadneedle Street, to regulate the affairs of a 'commercial resort' patronised by those trading to the Baltic Sea. This was seen as the start of what became the Baltic Exchange.

The present book marks the action taken eighty years earlier, in 1744, which led to those subscribers being almost exclusively involved in the Baltic trade. That was the naming of the same coffee house by its new proprietors as the 'Virginia and Baltick', whereas it had been known up to then as the 'Virginia and Maryland'.

In that first book I had an eight-page bibliography listing all the books and manuscripts I consulted, among them the short history of the Exchange written by its first secretary, J A Findlay, published in 1927. I have not referred back to any of these sources but have merely condensed the story I wrote, covering events from the arrival of the Lombard traders to Lombard Street in the fourteenth century up to the end of World War 2 (with a postscript to 1974), into a quarter of the space as Part I.

I have not interviewed again any of the many people I talked to in 1970 and 1971, whose names I listed on pages xv to xvii of the first book – with the happy exceptions of Mr Derek Walker, the secretary, who has only just retired; and of Mr Peter Harding of J E Hyde, who with Mr Tommy Turnbull, then chairman, was one of those most instrumental in keeping the exercise on the rails when, for various reasons, the publication date of 1973 was extended to 1977.

Today's chairman, Mr Peter Tudball, and the chief executive and secretary who succeeded Mr Walker, Mr Jim Buckley (and his personal assistant Mrs Sally King) have been my guides through the changed circumstances of twenty years on. For their enthusiastic help, and that of Mr Ted Owers and other members of the secretariat, and of Mr Hugh Renwick, membership adviser, I am very grateful.

My thanks are due to those who gave of their time to talk to me about aspects of the work of the Exchange with which they are familiar: Mr Philip G Soutter, Mr Frank Cordell and Mr Neil Rokison of Galbraith's Ltd; Mr Alan Bloomfield of H Clarkson & Co. Ltd; Mr Paul Vogt of Vogt & Maguire; and to those who, responding to the chief executive's request, sent me information regarding their companies which enabled me to give – from a random selection of potted histories out of a possible six hundred – an impression of the deep-rooted lineage of the enterprises that make up the tramp shipping community. These include Mr Andrew Olszowski, J S Hamilton Ltd; Mr Nigel P Ready, Cheeswrights; Mr Peter Talbot Willcox FICS, Eggar Forrester and Wilks Shipping Co. Ltd; Mr F M Everard, F T Everard & Sons Ltd; Mr Frank Major, Port of Sunderland Authority; Mr Bruce Farthing, International Association of Dry Cargo Shipowners; Mr James Sutcliffe, John Sutcliffe & Son (Holdings) Ltd; Mr David T Watkins, Stephenson Clarke Shipping Ltd; Mr John Good FICS, John Good & Sons Group; Mr Gary Weston, H Clarkson & Co. Ltd; Mr Erik van Oosten, Wijsmuller Holding BV; Mr J E Keville, Furness Withy & Co. Ltd; Mr Alan Bott, P & O Containers; Mr Stephen Rabson, P & O Steam Navigation Company; Moray Firth Maltings PLC; Mr P M Dodd, Erlebach Shipbrokers; Miss Margie Collins, Associated British Ports; Mrs M E Holmes, Anderson Hughes & Co. Ltd; Mr Richard Lund, Howe Robinson; Mr Eric Shawyer, E A Gibson Shipbrokers Ltd; Mr David Frame, Usborne PLC; Mr Richard Ottaway MP; Mr John Brady, Louis Dreyfus Trading Ltd; Mr Geoffrey Oswald, James Richardson & Sons; Mr Michael Peraticos, Pegasus Ocean Services Ltd; Mr M B Patrick, West Hartlepool Steam Navigation Co. Ltd; Captain Michael H F Smith, Master Mariner; and Mr Basil Fehr CBE, Frank Fehr & Co. Ltd.

I acknowledge making considerable use of information in articles and interviews in *Lloyd's List* and in *The Baltic* magazine, the lively new publication edited, since its launch in the spring of 1992, with great flair by Mr Deep Singh of Stroudgate PLC.

Finally I am indebted to the editorial committee appointed by the board to read and comment on the manuscript in draft for their helpful observations: Mr Eric Shawyer, Mr Alan Harper, Mr Adrian Stow, Mr Andrew McGovern, Mr Alan Hammond and Mr Jim Buckley.

H B-K
Ticehurst, East Sussex
November 1993

INTRODUCTION

In the seventeen years since Hugh Barty-King published his encyclopedic work on the history of the Exchange massive change in both the institution and the market has occurred. The remorseless march of ever more rapid communications, coupled with the fax and electronic mail, has set the seal on the traditional ways in which shipbrokers worked. At the latter part of the period, the swing away from commodities as the main thrust of the Baltic was completed when the various futures markets finally left the Floor in 1991 and were amalgamated into what is now the London Commodity Exchange. The centrepiece of the Exchange, the Floor, was becoming used less frequently. Separate morning and afternoon sessions disappeared and by the mid-1980s the market on the Floor was for an hour or so at lunchtime.

Twice during this period the Exchange strove to reposition itself both physically and strategically. In the mid-1970s the board of directors were on the point of recommending to shareholders that the Exchange be sold and a new site in Cutler Street be acquired, with a view to developing a group of exchanges, linked particularly to commodities. Subsequently, between 1987 and 1990 the Exchange obtained planning consent for the development of its building, which had now become listed by English Heritage, so that improved office accommodation to provide rental income to sustain the services to members could be obtained.

For a variety of reasons, neither of these bold moves was to be successful and by 1992 a dramatic cross-roads was reached.

But all this moves us forward too quickly. Hugh Barty-King spells out, in a tightly written first part to this book, the centuries of development that took the institution from Leadenhall Street to the Royal Exchange, Threadneedle Street and, at the turn of the century, St Mary Axe. His story up to that point focuses on the institution and its decisions. In the second part, the emphasis is on the market, with the companies and people who form that market centrestage. So, this part of the book gives us an impression, in a series of vivid cameos, of key players and companies in what has become the London bulk freight market, at the centre of which stands the Baltic – partly as a physical building but more importantly as a somewhat intangible, perhaps even mysterious, cement which binds together the membership. That cement is an admixture of received business ethics, regulation and, above all, a sense that from Baltic members the best commercial information will lead to the most profitable and secure deals for the bulk freight market.

Now, there is a blank page ahead waiting to be written on, and many would

Threadneedle Street looking west, showing the old coffee house.

question what future role the Exchange may have. When, decades ago, business could only be transacted by a physical appearance on the Floor, regulation by one's peers was easy and immediate. Transgressions — whether through sharp practice or over-enthusiastic but ill-advised pursuit of business ignoring the mostly un-written code of business ethics — would be pounced on and dealt with summarily.

As business has moved away from the physical market-place first to the humble telephone, then to the telex and the fax, and now to the all-pervasive screen — accessing informa-tion, transmitting and receiving messages and firmly shackling the broker to a desk — there must inevitably be a debate about the future role of the Exchange and its ability to continue to regulate a market which generates around US $¾ billion in commissions from charters, commodity deals and buying and selling ships.

To those who would argue that the dinosaur ultimately becomes extinct, the answer is given by the new direction set by the Exchange in seeking a redeveloper of its historic site whilst finding more modern premises on a more modest scale, to serve its members more effectively.

Key amongst the motivators for the new direction are the determination to take a more assertive stance on ensuring that the market is both professional and regulated; adding value through better information for members; and provision of appropriate meeting places and 'refreshment rooms' — as they were styled in 1900 — to allow the flow of information so vital to the transactions which move the world's raw materials.

It is too early to say whether this bright new vision can be sustained. It will only be so if it meets the business needs of members, and potential members, of the market. In commissioning this updated short history of the Exchange the directors and staff are determined that our history will be a springboard for the Baltic of the future.

J Buckley
Chief Executive and Secretary, The Baltic Exchange
March 1994

PART I

WHERE MERCHANT MET CARRIER

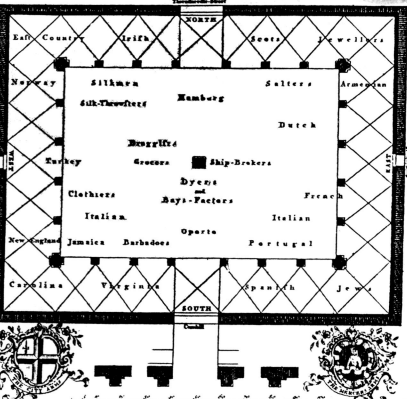

THE ROYAL EXCHANGE, was first built with Brick, at the sole Charge of Sr. Tho. Gresham, who laid the Foundation the 7. of June 1566: and was finish'd in Nov.r 1567. On the 27. of Jan.y following Q. Eliz. came to view it, and caused it to be proclaim'd the Royal Exchange. But being consum'd by the dreadful Fire in 1666, was rebuilt with Portland Stone, by the City & Mercers Company, & cost 50,000£ K. Charles II. laying the first Stone. It is now esteem'd the most beautiful, strong and stately Building of its kind in Europe.

THE PLAN shews the Area of the several Walks usually frequented by the different Merchants & their Factors from all Parts and is about 156 feet to the Long & 121 feet broad: in which more Business is transacted than in any other Place of its Compass in the known World. The Advantages to Traders with the Decorations which beautify this Royal Edifice, are too numerous to be described in this Place. Business is carried on here from 12 till 2 every day in the Year, except Sundays and some few Holidays.

NORTH

East Country · Irish · Scots · Jewellers

Norway · Silkmen · Salters · Armenian
Silk-Throwsters · Hamburg
Dutch

Druggists
Turkey · Grocers · Ship-Brokers · Portland's Key
Dyers and Bays-Factors
Clothiers · French
Italian · Italian
Oporto
New England · Jamaica · Barbadoes · Portugal

WEST · EAST

Carolina · Virginia · Spanish · Jews

SOUTH

Cornhill

THE CITY ARMS · THE MERCERS ARMS

Scale of Feet

ONE

TAKING THEIR TIME

for coffee, talk and news

This plan, drawn beneath the elevation of the first Royal Exchange of 1567 (left), shows 'the several Walks usually frequented by the different Merchants or their Factors from all parts' from twelve o'clock to two: shipbrokers in the centre, East Country at top left, Carolina and Virginia at bottom left.

When England declared war against her commercial rivals the Dutch in 1652, the sea battles cut her off from East Country goods, the important naval stores such as pitch, tar, hemp, timber and masts which she shipped from the countries bordering the Baltic Sea. So the Navy Commissioners looked to America for masts, to the pine forests of Maine and New Hampshire – to the plantations. Merchants who left the Virginia Walk on the Royal Exchange to continue their business in the tavern that had opened across the way in Threadneedle Street in 1603, signposted as the Virginia Wine House, drank to a turn of events which brought them the trade that for so long had been the mainstay of their colleagues on the East Country Walk.

In line with the fashion started by Kitt Bowman in St Michael's Churchyard off Cornhill at the end of the seventeenth century, the proprietor of the Virginia Wine House – while continuing to serve claret, arrack, rum and brandy in the vault below – saw fit to serve coffee to any customer who wanted it on the ground floor.

Coffee houses became the commercial resort of merchant and shipping men before and after attendance at the Royal Exchange and in between visits to the counting houses which were their offices. The proprietor of a City tavern or coffee house aimed to associate his establishment with a particular Royal Exchange Walk – with one trade. He rightly judged that people would be more likely to visit him regularly if they could rely on meeting others of the same trade – with common topics of conversation and shared contempt for the big, statute-protected trading companies – and wished to scan the same news-sheets for the same commercial intelligence. In the relaxed ambience of the coffee house, their business acquaintances became friends – friends they could trust.

The Virginia Wine House became the Virginia Coffee House and, for

1

a brief period in the spring of 1743 – to reflect the volume of trade with the plantations – the Virginia and Maryland (the latter being the adjacent state). But then another bout of sea warfare made the American seas too hazardous for British merchant ships. This time the challenge to Britain's free tramping of the seas came not from the Dutch but the Spanish, who had started visiting and searching British ships sailing to and from the British plantations, and were claiming the power of doing so as a right.

After an English squadron in the Mediterranean made prize of two Caracas ships, Britain declared war against Spain 'amidst the acclamations of the people'. And when, in April 1744, the King of France declared war against the King of England, George II could not do other than formally declare war against Louis XV. 'You may depend upon my endeavours', said the King of England on announcing his decision, 'to make this war as little burthensome as possible'. But the accounts which began to appear in *Lloyd's List* soon brought home to those who read them in the comfort of the Virginia Coffee House how very burdensome war at sea could be for those who sailed the oceans in the peaceful interests of trade.

Merchant with merchandise meets carrier with cargo space.

> **April 17, 1744.** The *John*, Captain Grey, from Maryland arriv'd at Weymouth, fell in with 13 Sail of French Men of War the 7th instant in Lat. 48–13, but it being a hard gale of wind he got clear of them again.

> **June 1, 1744.** The 26th of May at 6 o'clock in the morning being within sight of the North foreland, a Dogger Privateer, suppos'd to be French, belonging to Dunkirk, bore down and went three times round the ship *Lydia* of London, James Abercrombie Commander, from Rotterdam bound for South Carolina with Palatine passengers, and having kept company till the 27th in the morning, she then came within gun shot, being mounted with 14 carriage guns and seem'd to be full of men; but upon the *Lydia*'s crew and passengers giving three huzzas and firing a gun at them, they thought proper to sheer off.

For the British Navy to contain the situation, the Navy Board had urgent need to lay hands on naval stores of every description, in spite of the inevitably higher prices charged because of the greater risks involved in every voyage.

The principal suppliers were still the plantations and the East Country – the Virginia merchants and Baltic merchants. To the shrewd proprietors of the Virginia and Maryland it seemed commercially advantageous that they should cater specifically at 61 Threadneedle Street for those whose trade the war had thrown into such prominence, and from 24 May 1744 they changed the sign outside to read:

THE VIRGINIA AND BALTICK COFFEE-HOUSE

That day they put the following advertisement in the *Daily Post*:

This is to give NOTICE,

THAT the House late the Virginia and Mary- land Coffee-House in Threadneedle-Street, near the Royal Exchange, is now open'd by the Name of the Virginia and Baltick Coffee-House, where all Foreign and Domestick News are taken in ; and all Letters or Parcels, directed to Merchants or Captains in the Virginia or Baltick Trade will be carefully deliver'd according as directed, and the best Attendance given, by

REYNALLDS *and* WINBOULT

Note, Punch made in any Quantity, in the greatest Perfec- tion, without Adulteration, which is seldom found in any of the most noted Houses ; also Brandy, Rum, and Arrack (neat as imported) are sold in the Vault under the Coffee-House, at the lowest Prices ; where all Customers, we have had the Favour of serving at our late Warehouse in Leadenhall-Street, we hope will continue to send their Orders as above.

We have receiv'd Advice, that several Bags of Letters and Parcels are coming which are directed to be left at the above Coffee-House, ——— JACK from GRIGSBY's.

Reynallds and Winboult were a firm of wine merchants who once had cellars in Leadenhall Street and had taken over the wine vault under 61 Threadneedle Street. At street level they served chocolate and coffee to any who cared to enter. Theirs was an open house, a public house, with merchants and ships' captains in the Virginia and Baltic trades as regulars. However, there was no formality, no hint of anything resembling a club.

But just as the opening of Edward Lloyd's coffee house in Tower Street, whose supply of ships' news attracted those concerned with the business of indemnity and insurance, was the birth of Lloyd's of London, so the opening of the Virginia and Baltick Coffee House can be said to be the birth of the Baltic Exchange of London.

There was a dearth of coffee houses in the immediate vicinity of the Royal Exchange following the fire that began in a wigmaker's shop in Exchange Alley one afternoon in 1748. It destroyed many that had been rebuilt after the greater fire of 1666, including Garraway's, Jonathan's and the Jerusalem in Fleece Passage, Cornhill (Cowper's Court), frequented by gentlemen in the service of the East India Company and the managing owners of ships employed in their service, as well as merchants and policy and insurance brokers.

Neither the Royal Exchange nor the Virginia and Baltick Coffee House was damaged by the fire of 1748; indeed the rooms of the latter became more crowded than ever from having to cater for those who waited for the rebuilding of their regular haunts, such as the Marine Coffee House. The increase in the number of customers reflected the growth in Britain's population. Between 1700 and 1750 it rose from 5½ million to 6½ million, and in the second half of the eighteenth century it shot up to nine million, an increase of 52 per cent. Apart from that, the Baltic trade expanded. In 1810 the Commercial Dock Company obtained an Act of Parliament to buy the Greenland Dock and the adjoining Norway Dock, and convert them into a new East Country Dock to relieve the Thames of ships laden with timber, hemp, flax, pitch and tar, securing for the cargoes the benefits of lower insurance rates against pillage of the kind that was taking place in the northern docks. In 1809 one Joseph Moore and others formed the Baltic Dock Company to acquire a 45-acre estate at Rotherhithe on which to build pounds for storing and bonding timber.

Britain was engaged in an even fiercer struggle with the French than in 1744. This time it was with the seemingly invincible armies led by the general who had made himself their emperor. But Napoleon's well-disciplined troops, who won victory after victory on land, could never affect the control which Britain's navy had of the sea, which still relied to so large an extent on an uninterrupted supply of naval stores organised by the regulars of the Virginia and Baltic (the 'k' had been dropped by the 1790s). What William Pitt called Britain's naval greatness was no mere showing the flag or arrogant patrolling of the oceans, but a vast fleet of merchant ships protected by armed escorts, if need be, should any power take it into its head to challenge Britain's supreme position in the carrying trade of the world. England's great mercantile navy went about its business virtually unhindered, while the merchant fleets of France, in the words of Admiral Nelson, 'were shut up in her ports and could not send a cockle boat to sea'.

At the height of the war with the French in 1810, the Virginia and Baltic Coffee House on the easterly portion of No. 61 Threadneedle Street closed. It reopened three houses to the west at No. 58, which for two hundred years had housed the Antwerp Tavern. Its new proprietor was a wine merchant called William Melton. He removed 'Virginia' from the title so that the resort was styled the Baltic Coffee House, to which the custom of the Virginia and Baltic was transferred. It had no connection seemingly with the Baltic Coffee House listed in a 1765 directory as being at No. 6 Sweetings Rents/Swithins Rents, which ran along the east wall of the Royal Exchange and may not have lasted after the 1780s.

That William Melton decided to drop 'Virginia' and not 'Baltic' indicates a confidence in a present and continuing role for a Baltic trade which was fully justified, though in 1810 the war made it a trade of considerable danger. A shipowner had not only to put guns on board but also to insure against enemy risks, which became part of the conditions of hire and terms of carriage on which a merchant chartered a ship. The paper deed or charter on which these conditions were written was divided into two parts, and for this reason was known in medieval Latin as a *charta partita* and in French as a *charte partie*. It was a mutual covenant of which there were two copies, one for the merchant who 'chartered' the ship and one for the owner of the ship. The English version of the word is a corruption of the French, entering the language as 'charter-party' – or,

Charter-party of 26 July 1813 for the voyage of the Jaines carrying tallow to Archangel (right), witnessed by shipbroker James Bentley whose firm became Harris & Dixon, still in business in 1994.

Charterparty.

LONDON, *26 July 1813.*

IT is this Day mutually agreed between *Mr John Scott Owner* of the good Ship or Vessel, called the *Saines* of the Burthen of *212* Tons, or thereabouts, now *in the River Thames* and *John Ord Esqr for and on behalf of himself & Partners under the firm of Scott Ord & Co of London* Merchants;

That the said Ship being tight, staunch and strong, and every way fitted for the Voyage, shall *& will set sail on or before the second day of August next ensuing (if required) to Archangel or as near thereunto as she may safely get and there receive on board from the agent of the said Freighters a full and complete Cargo of Tallow, and other Goods but not less than Four hundred and ninety tons of Tallow*

which the said Merchants bind themselves to Ship not exceeding what she can reasonably stow and carry over and above her Tackle, Apparel, Provisions and Furniture; and being so loaded; shall therewith proceed to *London.*

—————————— or so near thereunto as she may safely get, and deliver the same on being paid Freight *at & after the rate of Seven Pounds & ton of weight for Tallow and for the Goods in the customary proportion thereto with Five Pounds & cent on the Amount of the Freight in lieu of Primage & Port charges*

——————————— *(The Acts of God, Kings enemies, Fire Restraint of Princes and Rulers during the said Voyage always excepted.) The Freight to be paid on unloading, and right Delivery of the Cargo, *One half in Cash & the other by Bills at three months.* Twenty running Days are to be allowed the said Merchant (if the Ship is not sooner dispatched) for loading the said Ship, at *Arch angel and Fifteen days for unloading London*

And *Ten* Days on Demurrage, over and above the said laying Days, at *Seven* Pounds per Day. Penalty for Non-Performance of this Agreement *£2000:*

John Ord

Witness Larver Bennett
Brother

as in the deed of 26 July 1813 drawn up by shipbrokers Burton & Bentley, all in one word, 'Charterparty'.

Golan Burton had set up as an insurance and shipbroker in Wapping in 1797 and was joined in partnership by his nephew James Bentley in 1810. In 1841 Burton & Bentley became Bentley, Harris & Dixon. When James Bentley died in 1846 the firm adopted the name of Harris & Dixon and was still operating in 1994 – the oldest firm of shipbrokers in London.

The 1813 charter-party beginning 'It is this day mutually agreed' has been the basis of many subsequent documents. After the printed words 'That the ship being tight, staunch and strong and every way fitted for the Voyage', were inserted particulars of the sailing date and of the 490 cases of tallow which were to be carried which 'the said Merchants bind themselves to ship not exceeding what she can reasonably stow and carry over and above her Tackle, Apparel, Provisions and Furniture'. The price charged for carrying the tallow – the 'freight' – was £7 a ton; twenty days were allowed for loading at Archangel and fifteen days for the *Jaines* to unload in London. Above the printed sentence 'Restraint of Princes and Rulers during the said Voyage always excepted', was added in hand 'The Acts of God, King's enemies'. The final sentence read, 'And *Ten* Days on Demurrage over and above the said laying Days at *Seven* Pounds per Day. Penalty for non-performance of this Agreement £*2000*.' The figures in italics were inserted by hand.

Tallow (animal fat) had an important role in Britain's commercial life. For a long time it was the only source of lubrication and a main source of light. Making tallow candles was an old trade. A guild of tallow chandlers had been formed in the fourteenth century. Tallow was a leading commodity, imported from St Petersburg, Riga and Archangel. 'Ton Tallow' became the standard unit for measuring all types of freight – and for calculating the price to be charged for carrying that cargo by sea. Merchants who specialised in tallow formed a group called the London Average Market Letter Committee. Their letter acted as a guide for merchants in the tallow trade. It gave a table of average prices fetched by tallow of various qualities during the previous week. A letter of October 1795 showed prices ranging from 7s[1] to 12s 4d a stone. Such fluctuations in price tempted many to speculation of a kind frowned on by others. The leader of a flash set who aimed to make big profits by taking advantage of cheap money and fluctuations in the price of commodities such as tallow was Richard ('Dicky') Thornton. He would buy all the tallow he could lay hands on, and keep it in store until the price rose and gave him a vast profit. Thornton once bet a Greek merchant £10,000 to £1,000 that Consols would not go below £85 in five years, and offered all newly married members of Lloyd's 100 to 1 against their having twins. In his booklet *The City, or the Physiology of London Business* (1845) D Morier Evans said Dicky would take a 'risk' at Lloyd's for £7,000 or £10,000 with a good premium 'as readily as he would a few casks of tallow at the Baltic'.

Within a circle of Russia and Baltic merchants who regularly attended

---

1 Sums of money are expressed throughout this book in the usage of the time; pounds, shillings and pence (£sd) were used until decimalisation in February 1971.

the Baltic Coffee House there was growing resentment against the Thornton clique and a suspicion that successful speculation depended on sharp practice and far-from-straightforward dealing.

A Richard Dighton cartoon captioned 'A Scene on the Baltic Walk, Royal Exchange in November 1822' – the East Country Walk had changed its name to Baltic Walk – was designed to expose Thornton's unscrupulous dealings in tallow. The scene was presided over by a winged 'Old Nick'. One of the crowd of men in billycock hats, tail-coats and britches is saying 'I never was so ashamed of John Bull before.' Twenty years later Morier Evans was describing the Baltic Coffee House of those days as:

> an establishment of considerable notoriety from the large speculations which at different periods have been carried on among the subscribers who, representing the trade in so important an article as tallow, have followed under a certain position of affairs that course of dealing that, like transactions on the Stock Exchange, frequently terminated in the ruin of the parties concerned.

The simmering uncoordinated sense of revulsion came to the surface on 22 April 1823, when regulars who felt the most strongly about the activities of Thornton and his associates – which were bringing their coffee house into disrepute – met at No. 58 Threadneedle Street to discuss ways of closing ranks against the unwanted speculators. Twenty-three of them volunteered to serve on the committee which they decided to form to put the place on a new footing. Headed by Thomas Tooke, the Russia merchant who became a renowned economist, they consisted of tallow chandlers, Turkey merchants, soap makers, brokers and merchants of many kinds.

The meeting decided that to one room at No. 58 they would admit only those willing to pay a subscription for the privilege – this was the subscribers' room or Subscription Room. They would restrict the number of subscribers to three hundred, a firm being regarded as a single subscriber. Only six subscribers could be stockbrokers. If more than three hundred were to be admitted the change would have to be approved by a general meeting. No longer were people to walk over from the Royal Exchange, pay their penny and become a member of the 'club' for the day. The Baltic Coffee House, or rather the part of it which kept the coveted newspapers and commercial information, the subscribers' room, was closed to all but the chosen three hundred. The names of candidates for admission to the ranks of subscribers had to be recommended by six existing subscribers, and such recommendations had to be approved by the committee of twenty-three elected on 22 April from among those who attended that inaugural meeting. Individual subscribers were to pay 4 guineas a year and firms of two partners 6 guineas. A firm with more than two partners paid 8 guineas. Each subscriber had also to give an 'allowance for the waiter' – another guinea a year for individuals. Apart from the inner sanctum, the Subscription Room, they decided that 'a dining room and a sale room be provided for the accommodation of the subscribers and the public, and that wine, tea, coffee, chocolate and sandwiches be provided in the coffee room'. The Baltic Coffee House at this time therefore consisted of 'the Room', a dining room, a sale room and a coffee room. Anyone could walk in from the street and use any of

Dicky Thornton's unscrupulous dealings in tallow on the Baltic Walk inspired the cartoon of 1822 (overleaf) by Richard Dighton, and led to the formation in the following year of the Baltic Committee to regulate the activities of subscribers to the Baltic Coffee House Subscription Room.

these except the Room. The sale room was upstairs and had its own entrance in Hercules Passage.

Subscribers could bring a visitor to the Room, but he had to be introduced by a member of the committee, who had to write his name and place of abode in a book kept for the purpose. To prevent gate-crashers, they decided that there should be only one door for admission.

All these decisions were embodied formally in thirteen rules and regulations. It was the responsibility of the 23-man Baltic Committee to see that they were carried out. They met twice a month on the first and third Tuesday at two o'clock in the afternoon. Five members of the committee formed a quorum. If subscribers had anything to say about the way the coffee house was being managed, they had to persuade fifty of their number to sign a requisition asking the committee to call a general meeting and state the reason for the meeting. Apart from that, the committee had the power to call a general meeting at any time. They declared the Room open on the first day of May 1823. In it subscribers found thirteen English newspapers, two French and two German newspapers, the *Amsterdam Courant*, the *New York Paper*, *Lloyd's List* and the whole range of lists, directories, calendars, almanacks and gazetteers. Rule 10 laid down 'That Ship Bills connected with the Russian and Baltic Trades only be allowed to be displayed in the room.' The meeting would have been held with the agreement of the proprietor of the coffee house, William Melton, who doubtless approved the rules and helped to draft them. He probably also acted as head waiter.

The Room duly opened on 1 May 1823 and within the first few weeks the visitors introduced by subscribers included shipping men and merchants from Paris, Stockholm, St Petersburg, Marseilles, Amsterdam, the Canaries, Sydney, Antwerp, Gibraltar, Madrid, Hamburg, Madeira and Jamaica.

'The Baltic' was off to a good international start.

Within twenty years it was obvious from Morier Evans's description that the intentions of Thomas Tooke, and his fellow reformers who called that meeting in April 1823, had been fulfilled; it was now:

> a very snug little place managed under the superintendence of a committee of management in a highly creditable manner ... The whole arrangements of the place show a nice taste for economy and comfort, and there is no lack of one or the other. The attendants are obliging and civil, having an eye to the committee of management who are sure to take notice of any irregularity in this respect.

In the public sale room upstairs tallow and oil were offered at auction by selling-brokers. It was a long narrow apartment in which samples of what was for sale gave off 'a slight effluvia'.

> The dingy appearance of the place, besmeared with ink from the pens of the juveniles, or clerks in attendance for principals who are not buyers and who, from the age of twelve upwards, may be seen either marking the prices paid in their catalogues or designing figures after the antique upon the deal tables appropriated to their use.

The first event in the sale room of the Baltic Coffee House was a series of 'Sales by the Candle' on 9 May 1823 – this was the conventional method of auctioning goods at this time, whereby the lot being auctioned went to the largest bid at the moment a candle burned to the bottom and extinguished.

How far the action of forming a committee and drawing up rules for the Baltic Coffee House was the result of righteous indignation at the wilder aspects of speculation in Russian tallow, and how far it was motivated by the desire to create a closed shop to ensure fair shares all round, is difficult to say. There was, it seems, an element of sour grapes in it, an anxiety to keep outsiders from spoiling the market, a move to preserve the status quo for the less adventurous, who were unwilling to take too many risks. It would be interesting to know how many, if any, of the regulars of the Baltic Coffee House found themselves excluded from their favourite haunt on 1 May 1823 as a result of being unable to find six friends willing to recommend them as one of the select three hundred.

They were not prepared to increase the number of subscribers when they had the opportunity to do so in 1837, the year George IV's niece, Princess Victoria, ascended the throne. The general meeting of subscribers, called for 5 May of that year to redraft the thirteen rules and regulations of 1823, decided that they should now be designated members, not subscribers, and that their number should still not exceed three hundred.

Where St Mary Axe joins Leadenhall Street as it was in 1817. The church of St Andrew Undershaft, still standing in 1994, is at the corner.

They increased the size of the committee from twenty-three to thirty and severely tightened the conditions of admission to the Room. The need for six members to recommend the candidature of a new member gave way to the requirement for each individual or firm to be proposed by one member and seconded by another, 'to both of whom he or they must be personally known'. The candidate's name, firm, residence, profession or trade had to be inserted in the Book of Candidates, with the signature of the proposer and seconder. The book had to lie open for the inspection of members for at least a fortnight. The vague stipulation that the candidate also had to be approved by the committee gave way to a formal ballot. Under the original rules, all the partners of a firm were entitled to use the Subscription Room by virtue of their firm's membership. Under the new rules a firm's partner would not be given individual membership.

They decided to meet once a month instead of once a fortnight. A quorum of five members could ballot for any candidate proposed to fill a vacancy in the membership: one black ball in five would exclude a candidate. If ten members signed a requisition asking for it, there could be a second ballot. An innovation was that a member who left town for more than a month could introduce his clerk as a substitute, but the latter, however, had to be balloted for as if he were a new member. A new rule prohibited the exhibition of samples in the Subscription Room. They continued to restrict the number of members from the Stock Exchange to six.

In 1823 they gave themselves no way of getting rid of a subscriber who for any reason became 'undesirable'. In fifteen years there must have been occasions when they wished they had, for in 1837 they introduced the thirteenth rule:

> Members having the misfortune to fail, or who compound with their creditors, after the adoption of these Rules, to be by that act excluded from the Society, but to be re-eligible on the same footing as new Members, after they have obtained their discharge or settled with their creditors.

The use of the word 'Society' is significant.

After fifteen years the annual subscriptions remained the same, but included the allowances for waiters so in effect they were reduced. The name of any member or firm who, after written notice, neglected to pay a subscription during May and June would be placed over the mantelpiece of the coffee room on 5 July following. If the subscription was not paid by 1 August the defaulter ceased to be a member.

To these reasons for ridding the Subscription Room of a member was added a third. The new Rule 16 read:

> In case the conduct of any member, either in or out of the room, shall have been, or shall in future be, in the opinion of the Committee, or of any Twenty-five Members, who shall certify the same to the Committee in writing, derogatory to his character as a man of business, he shall be subject to expulsion (without appeal) by the Committee which shall be specially summoned for the purpose of considering the same; and provided a majority of at least two-thirds of the *whole* Committee at that time in London shall concur therein, such Member shall thereupon cease to be a Member, and the proportion of his Subscription from the time of his expulsion to the close of the year ending 30th April shall be returned to him.

Wisely, without attempting to define what they meant by conduct derogatory to a man of business, the Baltic Committee bravely declared themselves on the side of the angels, and set themselves up as arbiters of business ethics independently of the law and the judiciary – as most professions had already done – in the hope of establishing an élite with standards few could ignore and all would emulate.

A key figure in the commercial chain of trust was the broker. In London in 1837 his trustworthiness was vouched for by the Corporation of London. Under an order they made in 1818 the Corporation issued certificates to brokers which stated they had entered into one bond or obligation in the penalty of £1,000 for honest and good behaviour, and another 'with security in the penalty of £50 conditioned for the yearly payment of £5 upon every Twenty-ninth day of September' for the same. The Court of Common Council then admitted the person concerned as a broker within the City of London 'during the pleasure of this Court and no longer', and swore him in.

Of the seventy traders listed in the street directory section of *Robson's London Directory* of 1838 giving their address as the Baltic Coffee House, eight were 'Brokers, General and Commercial', seven were Russia brokers, one was an insurance broker and one a shipbroker. The rest were described as merchants. John Monger, the head waiter, bought the coffee house and the goodwill of the business for £2,000 when William Melton died of cholera after returning from a dinner celebrating the passing of the Reform Bill. The coffee house at No. 58 Threadneedle Street was from then on referred to by many as Monger's.

William Melton's son, also William, became a shipowner/merchant, went bankrupt, studied law, moved abroad and for a time before his death in 1880 was acting Chief Justice of the Gold Coast (now Ghana). William Melton Junior's son Ernest inherited from his grandfather the Baltic Coffee House Subscription Room's Visitors' Book and Rule Book of 1823, which he presented to the Baltic Exchange in the 1920s.

Under the new set of rules unanimously agreed to at the general meeting held in 1837 – under the chairmanship of Henry Cayley – Monger's was a coffee house only in name. The regulars of the tavern-turned-coffee house had transformed themselves into members of a society who paid for the privilege of being the sole users of a room where businessmen could consort as friends, and where they could find the information on which they all depended for the profitable running of their businesses in the rapidly changing world of the electric telegraph, steamships and railways.

The following year, as if to mark the end of an era, fire gutted the Royal Exchange. Lloyd's conducted their marine insurance business from the building, and the fire had started in their 'Captain's Room'. Within a week they found temporary accommodation a few houses away from the Baltic Coffee House at South Sea House, Nos. 38 to 41 Threadneedle Street. For the eight years during which London was deprived of the Walks on which the City's trade depended, the Baltic Subscription Room became more crowded than ever, and there was relief when the young Queen Victoria drove into the City in 1848 to open the third Royal Exchange which, recently restored, still stands in 1994.

For the three hundred members of the Baltic Subscription Room the most welcome aspect of the new era was the triumph of the free trade movement launched by Baltic member Thomas Tooke in 1820. The change came with the repeal in quick succession of the Corn Laws (in 1846), resulting in the wholesale shipping to Britain of corn, and of the Navigation Laws (in 1849), no longer necessary for the maintenance of Britain's maritime power and for so long fettering trade and industry.

'This night is to decide between the policy of continued relaxation of restriction or the return to restraint and prohibition', Sir Robert Peel told the House of Commons on 16 February 1846: 'This night you will select the motto which is to indicate the commercial policy of England. Shall it be "advance" or "recede"? Which is the fitter motto for this great Empire?'

He asked MPs to consider the advantage which God and nature had given them. They stood on the confines of Western Europe, the chief connecting link between the old world and the new. The discoveries of science, the improvement of navigation, had brought them within ten days of St Petersburg and would soon bring them within ten days of New York – the Atlantic telegraph was not to come for another twenty years. He continued, 'Our national character, the free institutions under which we live, the liberty of thought and action, an unshackled press, spreading knowledge of every discovery and of every advance in science, combined with natural and physical advantages to place us at the head of those nations which profit by the free interchange of their products.'

It was the change in policy of which those whose business was the seaborne carrying trade had despaired, and words such as 'free interchange of products' were music to their ears. Demand for the services of shipowners, exporting merchants and their brokers broke all bounds. Finding they had more applications for membership than vacancies, in 1854 the Baltic Committee raised the limit from 300 to 325. At the same general meeting, for the swifter conduct of their business, the size of the committee was reduced from thirty to twenty. Benjamin Lancaster, a director of Price's Patent Candle Company, who had been at the forefront of the anti-Thornton pressure group and was now ending his stint in the key position of honorary secretary, took the opportunity of making another review of the rules and regulations. In 1837 expulsion was only possible 'provided a majority of at least two-thirds of the *whole* Committee at that time in London shall concur therein'. In 1854 they ruled that a two-thirds decision of the quorum could lead to expulsion.

It was hoped that the friendly atmosphere of the Baltic Subscription Room would deter anyone so inclined from conduct derogatory to his character as a man of business, which would lead to his fellow members expelling him. During the thirty-four years of its existence the Room had provided what seemed to be an ideal setting for the exchange of confidences, the giving and taking of hints and the updating of information for dossiers of the kind some kept in their heads and others committed to paper – just as Baltic member W Stuart Lane of Lane Hankey did in his small green leather notebook with a metal clasp which he carried in his pocket wherever he went. But in 1857 the Room had one major drawback. With the expansion of the membership to 325 it

The coffee house which became the Baltic on the left side of Threadneedle Street was just below the figure 52 on the Ogilby and Morgan map of 1676 (below). John Rocque's map of mid-eighteenth-century London (right) shows at top right the site of Old South Sea House and below it the South Sea House that became the Baltic in 1857.

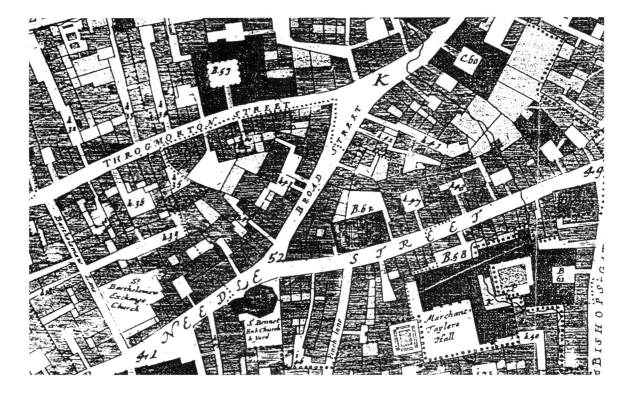

was nowhere near large enough. The snuggery in what had been the Antwerp Tavern in Sun Court had served its purpose for forty-seven years. Now, not only the waiting list but the prestige of the Baltic Coffee House called for a move to larger premises, ones which were capable moreover of allowing for even further expansion. The committee appointed a sub-committee of volunteers to examine the problem and make recommendations.

At this turning point in the life of the Baltic, the committee included two people with names linked with organisations of international repute. Pandia Ralli was the first of a family of Greek corn merchants and bankers who played a central role in the development of the Baltic. John Henry William Schroder was the son of the John Henry Schroder who came to London in 1804 and formed J Henry Schroder & Company in 1818.

What other buildings the sub-committee considered for the new Subscription Room is not known. Maybe they had a look at the Hall of Commerce which Edward Moxhay had built on the site of the French Protestant Church at 52 Threadneedle Street in 1843, but which never managed to attract as many subscribers as he had hoped. The building was reconstructed the next year and became Parr's Bank. It was demolished in 1921.

In 1855 the City was shocked by the failure of the Royal British Bank, whose major asset was the building it owned and partly occupied at the junction of Threadneedle Street and Bishopsgate Street – South Sea House, to which Lloyd's moved temporarily after the fire of 1838 had obliged them to abandon their offices in the Royal Exchange.

This was not the building used by the South Sea Company when it was formed in 1711. The company's first officers did their business in

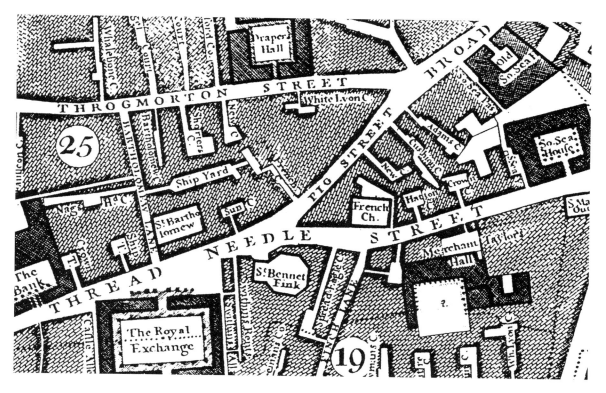

The South Sea House in Threadneedle Street which the South Sea Company built as their head office in 1732.

Merchant Taylors' Hall further west, on the south side of Threadneedle Street. Four years later they transferred to the large Excise House facing Broad Street and stayed there until 1720 – the year of the South Sea Bubble, which brought the company crashing down ignominiously with discredit and dishonour. Reconstituted as a whaling company, the South Sea Company leased a row of houses in Hammonds Alley on the north side of Threadneedle Street. In 1730 they demolished all the houses except one, and built on the big site a building of their own design. Completed in 1732, it was named 'The South Sea House'. The large Excise House, where they had rented a suite of rooms from 1715 to 1720, became known as 'Old South Sea House'. After being badly damaged by fire in 1826, it was pulled down, and in 1832 the City of London Club was built on the site.

To what extent the building owned by the Royal British Bank in 1855 was that built by the South Sea Company in 1732 it is difficult to say. Being more than one hundred years old, it is likely in any case to have undergone considerable alteration. Whatever the truth of the matter, its position, elegance and antiquity seemed to the sub-committee to make it an ideal choice for a new 'Baltic'. On 8 April 1857, by direction of the assignees of the Royal British Bank in bankruptcy, the leasehold of the South Sea House was put up for auction.

Its ground floor, claimed the auctioneers, contained 'the finest Banking Room in the Metropolis'. The upper three floors were let to sitting tenants, one of whom, appropriately, was the Russia Company. On the second floor three rooms were rented by the South Sea Company. At the auction the leasehold was sold to the bidder for the Baltic Coffee House.

A month after the auction on 8 May 1857, a company was registered with the name 'The Baltic Company Ltd'. Its objectives were to purchase the property known as the South Sea House, and to let the lower two floors to the subscribers to the Baltic Coffee House and other parts of it to other persons.

The nominal capital of the Baltic Company was £20,000. Its first shareholders were all members of the Baltic Coffee House Committee and included J H W Schroder and George Goss, a Russia broker who sometime between 1854 and 1857 had succeeded Benjamin Lancaster as honorary secretary. John Mollett, chairman of the coffee house's committee, was chairman of the company's fourteen-man board of directors, which included J H W Schroder, seemingly the prime mover of the whole scheme, George Goss and two Greek subscribers to the Subscription Room, Antonio Ralli and M E Rodocanachi. The formation of the company enabled the coffee house members to buy the leasehold of South Sea House, and share in its ownership, without individual liability in the event of the scheme failing to work out, as Edward Moxhay's had done. A third of the board also served on the committee. They appointed a full-time professional secretary to the Baltic Company, William J C Oxley, while George Goss remained honorary secretary of the Baltic Committee.

For John Monger the removal of the Baltic subscribers from Monger's was, as he told the committee in his letter of 23 July, a 'calamity'. He had been their servant and master, he said, for thirty-six years. Because the number of subscribers he catered for had grown, his landlords had raised his rent, and he had carried out considerable, and very expensive, alterations to meet their requirements. He was now upwards of 60 years of age and appealed to the charity and liberality of the committee to make provision for the future support of himself and his family, being suddenly and unexpectedly deprived of the goodwill of his business and the benefits he had hoped to realise.

No record has survived to show in what guise 58 Threadneedle Street spent its days before it became a post office at the end of the century. But that November, members agreed to compensate John Monger with 'one

The face of South Sea House changed only gradually. By the nineteenth century, as seen here, the railings had been removed and another storey added.

year's subscription' (although it is not clear what they intended by that), but their poorly done-by one-time manager had to write to them two months later reminding them of their promise.

The sub-committee who had organised the purchase told John Mollett that not only was the general accommodation very superior in every respect to what they had hitherto enjoyed, but that luncheon and dining rooms had been added for the convenience of members and a very excellent sale room had been built in connection with the Subscription Room but totally detached from it.

The company gave the committee an annual sum of £1,000 for running the Room: 'Thus the full control of all matters connected with the admission of members and the internal regulations of the Subscription Room, is left in the hands of the Committee of Subscribers while they are freed from pecuniary risk and responsibility.'

The old committee of management resigned. They trusted that their labours with regard to the arrangements for the move met with members' approval: 'They have been somewhat more onerous than most of us at the outset had anticipated, but if the New Baltic keeps up and extends the high standing for general energy, ability and integrity of its members, so long maintained by the old, they will not have been in vain.'

A new 'house committee' was elected which included eight members of the old one. They drew up new rules and regulations, the most revolutionary of which was to place no limit on the number of members – they would leave that until they had had the opportunity to ascertain the capabilities of the new Room. At their first meeting at South Sea House in November 1857 the committee were asked to consider the establishment of a court of reference for the settlement of disputes, but in the event they did not do so. They did rule, however, that the committee's decision to expel a member was not valid until it had been confirmed at a subsequent special meeting of the committee attended by at least twelve members, of whom three-quarters must vote in favour.

Another view of South Sea House, looking up Threadneedle Street, shows in the foreground more substantial iron gates beside a Post Office pillar-box.

At the first ordinary general meeting of shareholders of the Baltic Company in April 1858, it was stated that, although the directors had hoped there would be no difficulty in obtaining subscriptions from members of the Baltic for the two hundred £100 shares in the company, only 180 had been bought. Consequently expenditure had been in excess of capital. One reason had been the liberal expenditure in the refreshment department, another the large amount paid to the rector for tithes – 'a fearful burthen'. They now decided to purchase the freehold of the building and, to raise the required £47,775, they borrowed that sum, mortgaging the building as security for repayment. In fact they bought the freehold of South Sea House for £46,821 and raised a loan of £35,000 on mortgage from the Alliance Assurance Company for seven years at 4½ per cent, and another £12,000 by the issue of preferential 7 per cent shares redeemable in ten years. The annual charge, they reckoned, would be £2,437.

There were thirty-seven Greeks among the shareholders, including Pandia Theodore Ralli, Pandia Alexander Ralli, Eustrato Ralli, Michel Emanuel Rodocanachi, Leone Rodocanachi, Eustratius Ionides – who held three £100 shares – and Ambrose Theodore Ralli. The shareholders came from a wide variety of trades: there were indigo brokers, tar distillers, seed brushers, oil brokers, hide brokers, colonial brokers, corn factors, tallow dealers, ships agents, linen manufacturers, wharfingers, clerks, and at least one shipowner.

A new member admitted in 1858 was the 28-year-old Horace Clarkson, who had founded the firm which bore his name with Leon Benham in 1852. A name that dropped from the membership list was that of Thomas Tooke, who died in 1858 at the age of 84. He had been a prime mover in the formation of the Baltic Committee, now finding its feet in its new environment and learning to manage a membership which rose from 627 in March 1858 to 737 in March 1859.

The preoccupation of most of the members was trade with Russia. Communication was still mainly by letter, but at the end of 1858 they had the Magnetic Telegraph Company establish a telegraph office at South Sea House staffed by women and available not only to members but also to the general public. But when a member, George Dornbusch, who called himself a purveyor of commercial information, offered to supply the Room with Mr Julius Reuter's telegraphic services, the committee declined. When Reuter wrote personally from his office in the Royal Exchange proposing to inform them of arrivals at Liverpool and Southampton of the American, Brazilian and West Indian steamers several hours before the news was published in the papers, they deferred the matter 'to make enquiries'. That was probably an indication of their mistrust of yet unproven technology, though it was lack of funds which caused them to reject the later offer of Reuters Telegram Company to supply telegrams from New York, Havana, St Petersburg, Buenos Aires, Liverpool and Jamaica for £500 a year. They declined too to share the service and its cost with Lloyd's. Members such as the Ralli brothers, Glover brothers and Barings complained about the want of report of arrivals of vessels at ports and telegraph stations as posted at Lloyd's. They pointed to the transcript of Lloyd's arrival book kept at the rival commercial sale rooms and other subscription rooms: 'To obtain such early information as is necessary for the proper conduct of our business we are obliged to send specially to other places. We trust therefore you will afford us the same facility in our room.'

When forty members of the Baltic interested in the Australian trade petitioned the committee 'deeming it very desirable that reliable information should be obtained by telegraph from that colony, especially with regard to the shipments of produce', and asked for a monthly telegram giving particulars and statistics of the principal shipments, an agent of Reuters offered to supply the Subscription Room daily 'with the tone of the tallow market, prices of beef and mutton and copper for £20 a month'.

The wide-ranging nature of the commercial information required by members of the Baltic indicated that the interests of members were no longer confined to the Baltic Sea, northern Europe and southern Russia. By 1870, when the government decided that the country's telegraph system should be run by the state and the day of the private enterprise telegraph company came to an end, the sea-borne carrying trade of members of the Baltic was global. Members felt the service given by the General Post Office was too slow. In March 1870 Stephen Ralli called a special general meeting deploring the loss and inconvenience from delay and uncertainty in sending messages.

The General Post Office only took over British inland telegraphs, however, and those to Europe. The great network of overseas submarine telegraph cables – on which the global operators of the Baltic were now relying – was being laid by commercial entrepreneurs such as John Pender who in 1872 grouped his companies, which were already operating telegraphs to India, China and Australia, into his great Eastern Telegraph Company.

For Britain it was a period of unparalleled prosperity. There were only five industrialised countries in the whole world – the United States of America and the four European countries of Britain, France, Belgium and Germany. Together they accounted for four-fifths of the world's output of

The scene in the Pool of London when sailing ships had to start sharing the water with the steamships which, with the electric telegraph, changed the character of the sea-borne carrying trade which the Baltic served.

manufactures, and of that Britain had by far the largest share: 31 per cent compared with the USA's 23 per cent and Germany's 13 per cent. Britain's trade was worth £547 million, while that of France – the next largest – was only £227 million. The amount of shipping organised by members of the Baltic was proportionately enormous. It was big business, and those involved in it objected to the General Post Office calling the centre from which it was generated 'the Baltic Coffee House'. William Oxley wrote to the secretary of the GPO requesting that when their lists of postal telegraph stations were republished the place should be described as 'The Baltic'.

It was important that the outside world should have a correct image of what was being done at South Sea House. For the first time, in 1873, they produced a printed booklet, *The Baltic Rules and Regulations*, and a list of members. They were riding high. They increased the entrance fee from 5 to 10 guineas, increased the capital of the Baltic Company to £70,000, and declared a dividend of 30 per cent free of tax. The first printed list of members contained 1,164 names and included five Ionideses, six Mavrogordatoses, eleven Rallis, four Rodocanachis, six Schilizzis, and five Ziffos – these were a contingent of London Greeks whose contribution to the world shipping scene had for long been centred on Britain, as it still is in 1994.

The year 1873, in which trade had never been so good, was the jubilee of the formation of the Baltic Committee in 1823. No one, it seems, saw fit to celebrate it. And at least one member, Richard Wilson, saw it as the occasion on which to wonder whether they were overreaching themselves. In his letter to Oxley of 6 October 1873, thanking the committee for their expressions of goodwill following his resignation from it, he remarked that he need hardly say that he experienced much regret in withdrawing:

> I have served upon it for many years; and, during the whole time, my recollections in connexion with it afford me nothing but pleasure. I now retire because in my opinion – probably altogether a mistaken one – the committee undertakes functions which at a future time it may find it difficult and inconvenient to discharge.

TWO

CAMARADERIE AND MUTUAL GOODWILL

for corn traders; then tramp ship charterers

Although the Baltic Committee regarded suggesting ways in which members should settle their disputes as part of their remit, they saw the wisdom of not themselves becoming involved in any procedure members might adopt. They left the purely commercial matter of interpreting a contract (charter-party) or confirming a debt to independent 'arbitration' by an umpire or referee. On occasion, however, if invited, they would act as a court of appeal to give a second opinion. Often the arbitration clause in a contract would state that any arbitrator should be a member of the Baltic Committee, implying that anyone who belonged to it would be fair and impartial. But the committee, as a body, kept out of arbitration, though they frequently found themselves on the borderline. When Ruffles & Company appealed to them to help them recover £176 from Van Der Zee & Company, against whom they had started legal proceedings, they agreed to see Mr Van Der Zee and to examine the documents presented by Ruffles, a step which Richard Wilson might have considered beyond their terms of reference. They refused to give their collective opinion, however, and recommended Van Der Zee to submit the dispute to arbitration.

For the committee, agreeing to go to arbitration and then appointing a barrister as arbitrator was worse than refusing to go to arbitration in the first place. 'While distinctly disapproving of the refusal of Messrs Mesigh & Soule to appoint a Commercial Gentleman to act as their Arbitrator', pronounced leading committee member John Glover, 'a majority of the Sub-Committee is of the opinion that the circumstance does not necessitate the Committee taking action under Rule Ten' – the one about conduct derogatory to a man of business.

It was difficult to steer people away from the traditional reliance on documents and judgements which were 'legally binding' to the concept of binding themselves to others without the assistance of solicitors and

Many of those on the Baltic were Turkey merchants – such as Daniel Edwards, who in the 1650s introduced London society to the Turkish custom of drinking coffee. On the Floor they fixed trading voyages to and from the Ottoman capital of Constantinople (see overleaf) at a time when the first steamships were plying the Bosphorus alongside craft which could only move with wind and oars.

counsel, by assertions declared voluntarily as one man of business, and member of the Baltic, to another. To substitute 'my word', merely spoken, for the written bond with legal sanction, was to assume a climate of trust and openness in the existence of which cynics frankly refused to believe. Many were not prepared to take the risk. The committee had only themselves to blame if the concept was taking time to be accepted, for they were taking very few positive steps to propagate it, which was why there were misunderstandings and, on occasion, unpleasant imputations.

It was not a new idea. When in 1884 the Corporation of London planned to establish a court of arbitration, they pointed out in the printed circular they sent to the Baltic Committee, seeking their support, that they had 'during many centuries provided for the trading community of London various means of settling disputes by Arbitration'. It was difficult for people to understand that the point of *voluntary* arbitration was that it *was* unenforceable under the law, that it depended on both parties agreeing to stand by the arbitrator's decision *before they embarked on arbitration*, and that for this reason – as the City Corporation emphasised – it was swifter and cheaper than 'going to law'.

In February 1885 the Baltic appointed a sub-committee to report on complaints made to them of non-compliance by members of the Room with awards made under contracts. Their conclusion was 'that no complaint against a member of the Room arising out of an award shall be entertained by the Committee until the provisions of the arbitration clause of the contract under which the award was made are exhausted'.

Richard Wilson would probably have preferred them to spend less time passing judgement on members' behaviour, and more on tightening the procedures for withholding membership from people likely to become engaged in disputes and to react obnoxiously when they felt they had been unfairly treated.

By giving or withholding admission to the Room, the Baltic Committee could set the seal on a man's probity and creditworthiness, which the community at large would take to be lacking if entry were refused. By their power of expulsion for financial failure or acts derogatory to a man of business, they could virtually deprive him of that business. Their technique was to expel first and find out if it was justified afterwards. When a Mr Bellamy heard that his name had been removed from the list of members he wrote to the committee to ask why. The committee called him in and questioned him, and then resolved 'That Mr Bellamy's exclusion be confirmed.' They saw their job as having to apply the rules and make no exceptions. If a member's principal failed, so he no longer had a firm to represent, he ceased to be a member; and there could be no going back and arguing. And they applied the same rules to visitors to the Room as to members, which several members thought too severe and protested about in a petition. Overreaching themselves? Having to discuss such a criticism, decide whether to bow to it and have their decision submitted for approval to an annual general meeting, was certainly very time-consuming – as was having to rule on the disputes such as that between Julius Beerbohm, the member who published the *Evening Corn Trade List*, and Reuters Telegram Company.

Julius Beerbohm was a London grain merchant of mixed Dutch, German and Lithuanian extraction who became naturalised as British. His second son, Herbert Beerbohm, was elected a member of the Baltic in July 1874 and helped his father in his business at 28 Bishopsgate. Herbert devoted most of his spare time to amateur theatricals, became professional in 1878 at the age of 25, took the stage name of Beerbohm Tree and became one of England's most distinguished actor-managers. He built Her Majesty's Theatre in the Haymarket, founded the Royal Academy of Dramatic Art, was knighted in 1909 and died in 1917.

A matter about which the Baltic Committee had to make up their minds, of particular relevance to the ease with which members could conduct their business in the Room, was the vital one of communication.

When in September 1877 the engineer-in-chief of the Post Office received an invitation to a demonstration of a new invention from a Colonel Reynolds, the London representative of Professor Alexander Graham Bell, he declined it on the grounds that his department already had details of the professor's claims and that in his view the possible use of the so-called 'telephone' was very limited. So private enterprise took over. In June 1878 the Telephone Co. Ltd (Bell's Patents) was formed in London with an office at 36 Coleman Street. One of the first private telephone lines to be erected in the London area was from the Chiselhurst house of Henry F Tiarks, a leading member of the Baltic, to his stables.

It was a rival company, however, that made contact with South Sea House in September 1879. Arnold White, manager of the Edison Telephone Co. of London Ltd, in a letter to William Oxley, the secretary of the Baltic, told him:

> It is proposed to place the Baltic in direct telephonic connexion with those of the subscribers who may desire to communicate with their offices or with one another, without the necessity of writing or sending a messenger [a reference to the Exchange Telegraph Company, who ran a messenger service]. The instrument used is the sole invention of Mr T A Edison its conspicuous superiority over telephones consisting in the great range of its power.

White offered to run a wire from South Sea House to the offices of one or more of the sub-committee appointed to investigate the claims being made for the new invention. When they told him they would prefer to make the test on a line from South Sea House to the Corn Exchange in Mark Lane, he offered to do this without charge for six months' trial. To compare one with the other, the Baltic Committee also arranged for the rival Telephone Co. Ltd to give them a free six-month trial of a line to the Corn Exchange.

Members were far from impressed. With all the noise in the crowded Room they had great difficulty in hearing what was being said at the Corn Exchange, or in making themselves heard. They thought it would be better to give the pioneers time to overcome the teething troubles before wasting their money on a device that looked like being more trouble than it was worth. Improvement came with the amalgamation of the two rivals in 1880 as the United Telephone Company, and in that year some kind of instrument was installed with a line to the City's telephone exchange in Coleman Street.

The Room was not just crowded but overcrowded. In 1880 there

Overleaf: A montage of Baltic members in South Sea House about 1897.

were 1,239 town members and 98 country members, making 1,337 in all. In August of that year, in a petition to the committee, 380 of them complained of the total inadequacy of the accommodation and of the service. They strongly urged the committee not to renew the lease of South Sea House, which expired in May 1881, until some satisfactory arrangement was reached with their landlords the Baltic Company (which, though it had many outside shareholders, was controlled to a large extent by members of the committee they were petitioning).

The board of the Baltic Company told the Baltic Committee they were ready to make alterations to the building if the committee handed over £1,000 of their surplus funds and promised to renew the lease. When this was put to members at the annual general meeting in October, members rejected the proposals for alterations as 'quite inadequate' and instructed the committee to make the company submit a more comprehensive scheme. They rejected any idea of raising the 5-guinea annual subscription by another guinea. In December the committee sent a circular to members telling them that one way of alleviating the overcrowding was by renting from the Baltic Company the sale room at £1,300 a year, and using it as additional club premises; but this would mean having to raise the subscription to 6 guineas. The half of the membership who bothered to return the voting slip enclosed with the circular rejected raising the subscription by 272 to 220. It was back to the Room with all its inconveniences, except that members were now more fully appreciating the value of the telephone, which gave them immediate communication not only with their offices but with the specialist exchanges in other parts of the City that had taken the place of the Royal Exchange as the commercial resorts of shipping men and brokers.

That initial experimental line to the Corn Exchange was the most used. Most of the executive committee of the London Corn Trade Association were members of the Baltic. The LCTA had been formed by corn traders on the Baltic in 1878 to draw up such new forms of contract as they needed, to protect the interests of the corn trade generally and 'to select from its members a limited number of gentlemen of matured judgement and honourable character, with practical knowledge of the Corn Trade, to act as a final Court of Appeal in arbitration'. Its first contract form was for East Indian wheat, followed by a Black Sea and American form. Within six years they had uniform contract forms for most areas of the world.

The Baltic Committee had little alternative other than to renew their lease of South Sea House in 1881 for another seven years, and during that period it was the talk of the City that the strained relations between the Baltic Committee and the Baltic Company might end in a complete break. It was being said that they might leave South Sea House and take a lease of the Wesleyan Centenary Hall in Bishopsgate Street. Oxley assured Stephen Ralli there was no truth in the rumour. But at the end of November 1888 a group of members, led by F W Garrard and Seth Taylor, wrote a long letter to the Baltic Committee – who had just taken another seven-year lease of South Sea House – offering suggestions for terminating 'the existing state of tension between members and the Committee'. It was a matter which pressed for early attention, they said. It was less the demand of any section of members than the natural requirement of 'a vigorous and (consequently) developing community'. The key to future harmony, said Garrard, was to make the Room the

A bird's-eye view from Herbert Fry's London in 1886 *(right) identifies the Baltic Coffee House (centre left); the Wesleyan Centenary Hall at 17 Bishopsgate, a candidate for purchase in 1886; and, beside St Andrew Undershaft in St Mary Axe, the unnamed building which was demolished to make way for the new Exchange in 1901.*

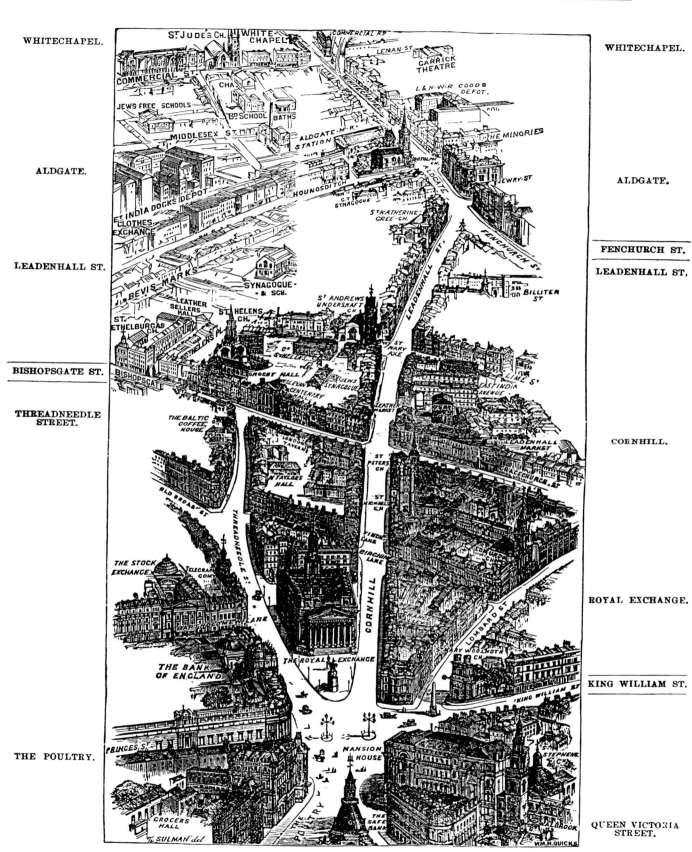

FROM THE POULTRY TO BISHOPSGATE STREET AND TO WHITECHAPEL.

property of the members, which meant increasing subscriptions and entrance fees to give an income of £15,700 from which to pay the cost of running the Baltic – £13,400 – and paying off his proposed debentures. Changing the subscription rates would mean changing the rules and regulations, and Garrard proposed rewriting them all and transforming the committee into another kind of body altogether, one which had the management and control of all matters relating to the Room, and of all the property and affairs of the Baltic.

William Oxley, who was secretary of both the Baltic Committee and the Baltic Company, was spared the dilemma of being seen to support one side or the other in this clash of interests, for at the beginning of April 1889 he died. He had given fifty years' service to the Baltic, for twenty-three of which he had been clerk of the Room or secretary. He was succeeded by Frederick Curtis.

At the committee meeting called to discuss the Garrard plan, the new rules – twenty-nine of them – which their solicitor had vetted were adopted. All that was needed for them to take the place officially of the old ones was a resolution of a general meeting to that effect. It seemed that at last the Baltic was steering into calmer waters. But then the four leading members of the Baltic Committee, who retired by rotation, withdrew their names for re-election. In the next few days Frederick Curtis received letters of resignation from four others, including Baron J H W Schroder, who also resigned his seat on the board of the Baltic Company. It was expected, ran the report of the committee that adopted the new rules, that the position of the committee would have been strengthened. However, owing to the retirements and resignations which followed, the reverse was the case. As a result the committee was reduced from thirteen to seven. Under the circumstances, the committee decided to postpone all proceedings with regard to carrying out the suggested new arrangements with the Baltic Company until the additional number of members required had been elected. Since that could not take place for another twelve months, the strain on the inadequate accommodation and services became greater than it had ever been.

The delay must have made the discontented angrier than ever. But the Baltic was not the only establishment of its kind. In December 1889 the shrewd manager of the Jerusalem Subscription Room and Exchange, built on the site of the 200-year-old Jerusalem Coffee House in Cowper's Court off Cornhill, issued a leaflet calling the attention of those who found South Sea House too crowded, and too expensive, to 'the numerous advantages this old-established City Rendezvous offers to gentlemen interested in Exports and Imports, Freights, Shipping and Mercantile affairs generally'.

'Change' was held there daily, attended by a large number of gentlemen interested in shipping and mercantile relations with the colonies, the Cape and the East, for the purpose of arranging freights and charters and generally transacting business. There they found the latest information about arrivals of vessels and mails from the west coast of South America and the north Pacific, notices of freight wanted, government tenders and lists of homeward-bound wool, wheat and nitrate ships. Important political and general news was received in the Room by wire and conveniently arranged for reference. There was a telephone in the Room for the use of members.

Most importantly, the entrance fee was only £2 2s and the individual annual subscription was only £4 4s, less than half the proposed subscription for the Baltic.

The obstacle to any enlargement of the Room at South Sea House was always the refusal of members to contemplate an increase in the subscription. Every year they admitted more members – the total in 1890 had climbed to 1,534 – every year the committee opened negotiations with the company, every year they were faced with the question of how to find the money needed to pay for the necessary structural alterations. It seemed that the Baltic would acquire a new sense of direction when, at the annual general meeting of 1891, William Bridges Webb of Dewar & Webb agreed to join the Baltic Committee, along with Seth Taylor of Harris Brothers & Company and Septimus Glover of Glover Brothers. When Bridges Webb moved that they suspend election of any new members for the time being – for the first time in the history of the committee – the resolution was carried by eleven votes to two.

The shipping trade journal *Fairplay* could not understand why, with the Baltic Company earning so high a rent income, more suitable accommodation could not readily be obtained. 'It is no news that for a long time there has been considerable friction between the Committee and the Company, and the question is whether it may not be for the interest of the company to give the accommodation required, rather than drive the committee to go elsewhere.' (13 November 1891)

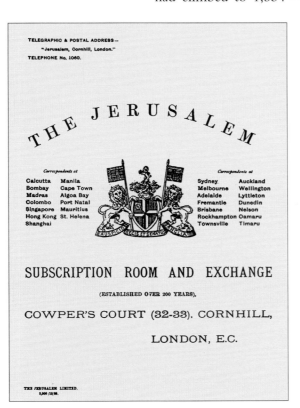

The front page of a leaflet issued by the Jerusalem in 1889.

Such an eventuality seemed more likely than ever. For, in addition to the Jerusalem, which they could join at once, many members of the Baltic would have been attracted by the announcement they read in the next issue of *Fairplay* of a meeting to be held just before Christmas in the Ship & Turtle to discuss the possibility of establishing a central shipping exchange for London.

In London, ran this announcement, shipowners and merchants or their representatives had generally to go from office to office to see one another, unlike on the Continent, where they could always be found in a *bourse*:

> London is too large for one central general Exchange, and the different sections of trade have founded their own Exchanges at centres convenient to them; but the shipping interest, which is not the least important one in the metropolis, has hitherto been without a business institution of its own. The 'Baltic' is a grain and grain-chartering market, and by no means representative of the shipping trade generally; and even as the home of grain-chartering it has become too small to accommodate properly the shipbrokers, charterers and others who flock to it.

The promoters of the new shipping exchange thought it possible that their institution might in time so develop as to afford suitable accommodation for those who now found the Threadneedle Street centre too limited. There was no idea, however, of setting up in rivalry with 'the famous and extremely fortunate' Baltic Company. They merely wanted to provide a more convenient meeting place for shipping business than existed and to establish improved facilities for discussing trade questions 'at present handled in so perfunctory a manner by the leisurely merchants and faddists who constitute the Chamber of Commerce'.

The London Shipping Exchange was duly registered in February 1892. The annual subscription was £3 3s and there was no entrance fee. The Exchange planned to accept the offer of the Ironmongers' Company to use the ground floor of Ironmongers' Hall as temporary premises for the first years.

That same month the directors of the Jerusalem Ltd announced they were closing their premises in Cowper's Court and opening a shipping exchange at No. 22 Billiter Street, which they had just purchased, and that they had plans for purchasing another site later on which to erect buildings 'which will be an ornament to the City'.

But then, the first London Shipping Exchange promoters, having second thoughts about moving temporarily into Ironmongers' Hall, took a lease of No. 19 Billiter Street for their centre, next door to No. 22, which they opened on 16 March. Two leading members of the Baltic, Theo Angier and Francis Lenders, joined the board of directors.

The seal of the new Shipping Exchange.

The new Jerusalem duly opened its doors, but it only survived for that spring and summer. When its directors sold the establishment to the London Shipping Exchange, No. 22 was closed and their members there were taken on by the club next door. The now consolidated London Shipping Exchange was opened by the Lord Mayor at Nos. 19, 20 and 21 on 30 January 1893, with the popular shipowner Sir Donald Currie as president.

The big Exchange floor was at street level, and upstairs were a luncheon room and a reading room. It was all lit by the new incandescent electric light, which gave it a very much more 'modern' look than the surrounding gas-lit houses. Some of the correspondents who attended the opening ceremony wondered whether the place was intended as a club or a business centre. Others pointed out that the lack of the facilities it provided had long been a drawback to London merchants. Glasgow and Liverpool already had them, as had many cities abroad. The founder of the London Shipping Exchange saw its opening as destined to form an epoch in the commercial history of London.

When it proposed closing its doors at Afternoon Change to ensure punctuality, many objected. If a shipbroker had a charter-party to negotiate subject to telegraphic reply by 3.45 p.m., he visited one merchant after another, finally concluded the charter – the fixture – sent off his telegram and went back to Billiter Street, where he would find the doors closed. If brokers frequently found themselves shut out of the Exchange, commented *Fairplay*'s Look-out Man, they might transfer their patronage to the Baltic.

But there seemed little fear of that. The London Shipping Exchange was an instant success, much of which must have been due to the strict regime established by the man whom Ernest Forwood and his colleagues chose to run the place as secretary and manager, James Arbuckle Findlay.

It soon had 1,500 members. The Baltic, it seemed, had been eclipsed. While all the wrangling had been going on between the property company and the committee, between committee and members, leading traders and brokers like Ernest Forwood and Alexander Howden had created the new Exchange in Billiter Street under their very noses. James Findlay and Frederick Curtis kept in touch, however, and Ernest Forwood corresponded with the chairman of the Baltic Committee, now Bridges Webb. The two bodies had an annual rowing match on the Thames at Putney. But there was no doubt that the popularity of the Baltic declined. In 1894 came the first decrease in the number of members since the Baltic Committee was formed in 1823 – 1,395 as against 1,448, a drop of fifty-three. This was largely due to the increased subscription for South Sea House which compared unfavourably with that for Billiter Street; the latter's was much smaller.

The next year 111 members of the Baltic signed a petition to the committee drawing their attention to the fact that, although a large proportion of members were engaged in the shipping trade, the information contained in the Room fell far short of that obtainable at any other leading exchange. Members interested in the grain trade, on the other hand, were fully supplied with telegraphic information.

Bridges Webb, a grain man, sought the advice of Colonel Henry Hozier, the secretary of Lloyd's, who suggested the information supplied in the Room at South Sea House should include important casualties, arrivals of grain steamers and sailing ships at Odessa and Black Sea ports, and of sailing vessels at Californian ports and steamers and sailing vessels at Australian ports. Hozier did not think, however, that the Baltic needed to introduce 'anything like the same amount of service as the Shipping Exchange'.

Information was the life blood of the Baltic a hundred years ago, as it is today, and the wider service introduced as a result of dissatisfaction felt in 1894, culminating in the following year's petition, to some extent appeased the Ralli brothers, J H Schroder, Theo Angier and the other signatories. The interests of shipping members were again furthered in 1895 with the holding of the first ship auction sales in the Room. These were by C W Kellock & Company of Liverpool, who had been holding them in the Captain's Room at Lloyd's. The firm was a member of the Baltic, however, and this was the beginning of a long series of ship sales conducted at the Baltic by Kellocks, who later moved to London.

But whether they were shipping or grain orientated, the 1890s generation of members was not as sensitive as hitherto to the delicate unformulated relationships on which, perhaps more than anything else, the reputation and tradition of the Baltic depended. People were blatantly introducing visitors who were the kind of people that would not be admitted as members. The privilege of introducing visitors was being grossly abused. The committee changed the rule so that if a member took to the Room someone whom he knew had been charged with conduct derogatory to his character as a man of business, he would himself become liable to suspension or expulsion.

Inevitably a minority admired the clever operator who succeeded in tricking a fellow member, who would never consider doubting the truth of his assurances. Sharp practice? Just being 'cute'. But, as John Wrenn said at the eighth Baltic dinner at the Trocadero:

neighbourly feeling, fair dealing and straight speaking have come to stay and increase and multiply among us ... With us dwells a decorum of demeanour which I think is above the average of most commercial concourses. Other and perhaps neighbouring institutions may have their bear fights and their bull fights, their cockpits and their corners, but the delicate dignity of the Baltic revolts at even the innocent innovation of a guileless grain ring.

Raising cargo from holds and lowering it into holds by derrick and crane, checking the number of barrels, weighing them and removing them to the store – as is being done in this busy nineteenth-

century scene – is still the routine at the heart of the business brokered on the Floor of the Baltic. Only the technology has changed.

It was with some justification that these hard-headed businessmen of one hundred years ago congratulated themselves on the extent to which, in the 150 years since the establishment of the Virginia and Baltic Coffee House, they had created the climate of trust which they and their successors were never to lose. If they were slower to cultivate – at least for their shipping members – the more materialistic aspect of their operation, the swift supply of up-to-date information, in 1895 they would have been glad to read of a technology that promised to add a new dimension to communication by telegraph and telephone. This was the invention by a young English telegraphist called G F Creed of a Morse keyboard tape perforator to actuate a typewriter mechanism, which led to the teleprinter and the network of teleprinters called Telex.

Such communication facilities and information as the Baltic Committee were willing to provide were geared for an institution which a writer in *Chambers Journal* in 1896 described as 'the great emporium in London for foreign grain'. Each part of the trade had its corner. In the centre congregated the linseed brokers; at the further end the traders in wheat and feeding stuffs.

> Produce valued at many thousands of pounds daily changes ownership without the production of a single document binding the bargain until the contract notes are drawn and signed. Confidence in mutual integrity after the conclusion of a bargain forms the basis of this apparently loose system, and anyone abusing this confidence, say by repudiating a bargain, would be reported to the Committee and upon conviction would be instantly relieved of his membership.

Near the entrance to South Sea House was 'the freight market', where no goods changed ownership, only the temporary occupation of a space inside a tramping cargo ship – in other words, the sea-borne carrying trade. Here the same mutual integrity prevailed, and the same ability to transact the maximum business with the minimum time and trouble.

Going on 'change' at the Baltic was the only way to conduct the business of buying, selling and transporting foreign grain. The circumstances in which the trade was conducted as the century grew to an end were changing, and to many it seemed that the London emporium in which it was conducted needed changing too. The latest seven-year lease of South Sea House expired in September 1899, and the committee, composed of a new younger generation, seriously considered not renewing it and looking for more commodious premises. Or, since the finances of the Baltic Company were in so healthy a state – their £100 shares were now valued at £700 – perhaps they could be persuaded to build members a brand new exchange of their own?

In November 1898 the committee engaged a separate solicitor and a firm of estate agents to advise them regarding a 'proposed new building', and set up a sub-committee to work out the details which met on Monday 6 December. As soon as James Findlay got wind of the Baltic's intentions, he wrote formally, as secretary of the London Shipping Exchange, to his counterpart at South Sea House, Fred Curtis:

8th Dec 1898

Dear Sir,

My directors have noticed in the Press that your Committee have under consideration the question of removing to other premises, and I have been requested to ascertain if they will receive a deputation from them to consider the expediency of bringing both bodies of Members under one roof.

Septimus Glover, the chairman of the Baltic Committee, duly met Ernest Forwood, who on 12 December wrote to Glover summarising the proposed idea which they had discussed 'of seeing whether some arrangement could not be arrived at that will enable the members of the Baltic Exchange and the members of the Shipping Exchange joining together and building an Exchange worthy of the City of London'.

Ever since I have been in London – some 28 years or more – I have found it irksome to have to attend so many Exchanges in order to carry on my business; I have also found it very costly in as much as I have to subscribe for my clerks being members both of the Shipping Exchange and the Baltic. Now, if anything could be done to concentrate the trade of the City under one roof it would prove a great boon to the City commercial world, especially seeing now that everybody has to get through more work in a day than was the case in the past.

He had studied all the sites in the City for two years and found that the only one which would give the area necessary for a general shipping exchange was in Jeffrey's Square, which was about 12,000 square feet with good light at three sides. He calculated that within twelve months of signing the contract, everything would be ready.

Jeffrey's Square lay between St Mary Axe and Bury Street to the north of Leadenhall Street. It was where Charles Dickens was to locate the offices of the Cheeryble brothers in *Nicholas Nickleby*.

The Baltic Committee discussed Forwood's letter on 14 December, and decided to ask Glover to send a letter in reply stating they were not at present free to consider the proposal, 'being somewhat committed in another negotiation'. This was a revival of the idea, contemplated in 1886, to buy the Wesleyan Centenary Hall at 17 Bishopsgate, which had once been the magnificent City of London Tavern which seated four hundred for dinner. Or should they renew the lease of South Sea House from the Baltic Company for another seven years, with members paying for alterations and repairs? A special general meeting of all members voted to give the committee full authority to do what they thought best in the interest of members of the Room. Those who favoured the Jeffrey's Square plan issued a circular signed by Forwood (a member of the Baltic) and others, and Fred Curtis authorised the posting of it inside South Sea House, an act considered so disloyal to the committee as to warrant censure of him. Curtis, finding his position untenable, resigned.

Two further ideas were put up: the purchase of Christ's Hospital in Newgate Street, once the Greyfriars monastery, becoming vacant on the move of the school out to new buildings near Horsham; or of a site facing Fenchurch Street Station offered by shipbroker James Dixon of Harris & Dixon. Both were rejected.

Jeffrey's Square, St Mary Axe, which the City of London Exchange offered to sell to the Baltic Company for £175,000 in 1899. It was pulled down and became the site of the new Baltic Mercantile & Shipping Exchange completed in 1902.

When Forwood was told that the Baltic's hesitation in taking up his offer was due to their belief that Jeffrey's Square was not on the market, he told Glover that he held a firm offer of the site in writing for fourteen days. He would be prepared, he said, during that fortnight to give the Baltic a firm offer to rent the proposed Exchange or to transfer the offer to them. The Baltic Committee once more held back, and wrote to Forwood that they did not see their way to taking any steps in the matter. So before his option ran out Forwood, with the aid of a group of friends, took it up himself. If the Baltic changed their minds again, and decided to buy the Jeffrey's Square site and build their own Exchange there, it would injure the Shipping Exchange, since it would enable them to offer such facilities and club comforts as would be bound to attract many Shipping Exchange members. So Forwood persuaded the Shipping Exchange to form a group to purchase the Jeffrey's Square site 'and create a new Exchange Company'. They called this 'The City of London Exchange Syndicate', which was registered on 6 June 1899.

The directors of the syndicate offered to sell the Baltic Committee the freehold of the Jeffrey's Square site for £175,000. They would transfer the property to the committee, 'leaving them to make the necessary arrangements for the building of the Exchange and the formation of the Company to acquire it', which would have a capital of £275,000. The committee needed more time, and instructed their secretary (now Charles Oxley, William's son) to write to the secretary of the Baltic Company, who was also Charles Oxley, for an extension of their lease of South Sea House. When the company refused, they sold the building to the British Linen Company for £350,800, and on 14 September 1899 the Baltic Company Ltd was wound up voluntarily.

The reading room of the Baltic at South Sea House – a photograph taken in 1900, two years before the Baltic moved from the building to St Mary Axe.

At the annual general meeting of members on 19 October Stephen Ralli moved that the Baltic signify its approval of the proposed removal to the new Exchange to be built in Jeffrey's Square, and give authority to the committee to agree terms with the City of London Exchange Syndicate. Only three voted against.

The year 1899, a turning point in the history of the Baltic, ended with the annual dinner at the Trocadero, 'the most effective *mise-en-scène* for the display of camaraderie and mutual goodwill which is so characteristic of the Baltic community'. William Weeks, the evening's chairman, proposed the toast of 'The Shipping Interests'. Though only a year before the Jeffrey's Square site was in the clouds, the Baltic would be safely anchored in St Mary Axe by September 1901. It was a statement, as *Fairplay* reported, received with cheers of hope mildly tempered by scepticism, while a shudder passed over the audience on the reminder that South Sea House would close its doors to members in September next.

Where to go while the new exchange was building? The Bishopsgate Institute? The Royal Exchange? Early in the new year a more attractive proposition came from Lord Hamilton of the Great Eastern Railway Company, who suggested members could have temporary use of the banqueting hall being built as an annexe to the Great Eastern Hotel at Liverpool Street Station.

The body that was to own and administer the Jeffrey's Square project was neither the fifteen-man committee of the unincorporated association of 1,250 subscribers known as the Baltic Committee, nor the property and investment enterprise the Baltic Company, nor the London Shipping Exchange, nor the City of London Exchange Syndicate. All agreed it had to be a completely new and separate body. As it would be a meeting place for both merchants and shippers, they decided to call it 'The Baltic

The foreign telegrams corner at the Baltic in 1900.

Mercantile & Shipping Exchange Ltd', and as such it was incorporated on 17 January 1900. It had a capital of £200,000. William Bridges Webb was elected chairman. He had entered the grain trade as a young man of 21 in 1870 and had become a member of the Baltic two years later. He was president of the London Corn Trade Association from 1896 to 1899. He had a commission in the Honourable Artillery Company and liked to be known as Major Bridges Webb. The object of the new company was to acquire the Jeffrey's Square site from the syndicate and build on it an exchange which would take the place of the Baltic in Threadneedle Street and the London Shipping Exchange in Billiter Street. They reckoned the property, when finished, would be worth £440,000 and the offices would yield a gross annual income of £18,900. With 1,350 members of the Baltic and 1,410 of the Shipping Exchange, they saw no difficulty in attracting the stipulated maximum membership of two thousand. The new company's purchase of the site from the syndicate was completed in April. On handing over a cheque for £87,693 to Ernest Forwood, Bridges Webb congratulated him on the successful outcome of efforts begun more than twelve months before. The contractors, G W Trollope & Sons, submitted an estimate of £171,130 for erecting the superstructure of the building, designed by W Wimble FRIBA and T H Smith, and undertook to complete the work in twenty-two months.

Top hats were de rigueur *on the Floor of the Baltic at South Sea House, where members (men only) did their business throughout the second half of the nineteenth century.*

The British Linen Bank were unable to delay their plans for demolishing South Sea House[1] to allow Baltic members a further stay when the building of the Abercorn Rooms at the Great Eastern Hotel took longer than expected.

The furniture and fittings of the Baltic at South Sea House were sold by auction on 1 October 1900. They included a Waygood passenger lift, a wind dial and a marble and silver plated fountain, 'the Ancient Chair for the use of the House Porter' and bound quarterly volumes of *The Times* from 1850 to 1900. On the day of the auction, members were carrying on the transactions which they were unable to complete at Threadneedle Street on Saturday in the great hall of the Great Eastern Hotel extension, which over the weekend had become 'The Baltic'.

The completion of the sale of South Sea House to the British Linen Company on 30 September was the last function of the liquidators of the Baltic Company. The final account showed the disposal of a sum of £366,217 of which £350,800 was for the sale of South Sea House. It

1 The building which stands on the site of 37 Threadneedle Street in 1994 was built in 1901 and no part of it belongs to the South Sea House which was the Baltic for forty-three years, nor was it ever the headquarters of the South Sea Company. It became the British Linen Bank, which changed its name in 1972 to the Bank of Scotland.

25 June 1901. The Lord Mayor of London, Frank Green, lays the foundation stone. In the top of the massive stone was inserted a lead box containing

showed £327,391 paid to stockholders since liquidation – 10 per cent on 24 October 1899, another 10 per cent in March, 37 per cent in October and a final 43 per cent in November. As the largest shareholder Michel Rodocanachi, with 1,400 shares, collected £11,102 – apart from his share of the £2,887 directors' bonus and £1,816 liquidators' remuneration, on which he paid a shilling in the pound income tax.

JUNE 25th 1901.
ALFRED ELLIS & WALERY.
Photographers.

newspapers and other articles from that day. This 'time capsule' was recovered in 1993 – see page 101.

Throughout the short period between the evacuation of South Sea House and the occupation of St Mary Axe, three bodies operated independently which were later to merge into one: the Baltic at the Great Eastern Hotel; the London Shipping Exchange in Billiter Street supervised by a management committee of the Baltic; and the Baltic Mercantile & Shipping Exchange with James Findlay in charge, supervising the building of the exchange in St Mary Axe and preparing for the new body that was to operate there. Seth Taylor, who took over as chairman of the Baltic Committee from Septimus Glover, and Bridges Webb formed committees to draw up a new set of rules.

These declared that no one was to be eligible for election as a member, other than a British subject, until he or his firm had been domiciled in the UK for twelve months. The board of directors of the Baltic Mercantile and Shipping Exchange were given the power of censuring, suspending or expelling a member 'who, in their opinion, has been guilty of improper conduct or who shall make use of the Exchange for purposes other than the proper purposes thereof, or who shall have violated any of the rules or regulations, or who shall have failed to comply with any of their decisions'. They were empowered, most importantly, to notify other members or the public that they had expelled or suspended a member, which was not actionable in law by that person against the board. Complaints against a member had to be made to the chairman in writing. If a non–member made a complaint against a member, the directors would hear the case if they considered it fit for their adjudication, and would have the complainant sign a written consent binding himself to carry out their award before the hearing began, as if he were a member. Moreover, he had to promise not to prosecute or take part in any civil or criminal proceedings in respect of the case.

By the time they had hammered out the framework of a constitution, the Lord Mayor of London, Frank Green, had, on 25 June 1901, laid the new building's foundation stone. The ceremony was followed by a luncheon in the hall of the Merchant Taylors' Company, of which Seth Taylor was master. The royal toast was to the country's new monarch, King Edward VII, who had succeeded his mother Queen Victoria on her death in January 1901.

When it was obvious that the new exchange would never be ready by 15 January 1902, which Trollope & Sons had given as their completion date, the Great Eastern Railway gave the committee an extension of the Abercorn Rooms to 31 March 1903.

Seth Taylor presided over the last annual general meeting of members of the old Baltic at Winchester House on 16 October 1902, when he found time to refer to the formation of the Baltic Rifle Club, prompted by the military training everywhere in evidence for the war that had been waged against the Boers in South Africa since October 1899. Before the year was out James Findlay, as secretary, was laying plans for the opening of the new Exchange on Tuesday, 21 April 1903. The first batch of London Shipping Exchange members, some 680 of them, were formally elected members of the Baltic at the beginning of April; the last ship sales were held at Billiter Street and the Baltic Committee made arrangements to abandon the Abercorn Rooms. Only the ground floor was ready when three thousand members and their friends saw Major Bridges Webb, Ernest Forwood and other directors escort Sir Marcus Samuel, Lord

The end of the room

Mr Seth Taylor

Mr E. Forwood

The Lord Mayor declaring the new exchange open.

Mayor of London and a member of the Baltic, to the dais inside the colourful marble Floor on 21 April to declare the reconstituted Baltic Exchange open. He hoped that a great and noble career of usefulness was open for the Exchange, dedicated to the advancement of commercial and friendly relations with its world-wide connections and the development and consolidation of international concord:

The opening ceremony of 21 April 1903 – a sketch in Shipping World *which included, bottom left, a portrait of Ernest Forwood, the prime mover of the whole project.*

> Commerce and mutual interest have done, and are doing, more to draw nations together than all the artifices of diplomacy, and these peaceful achievements of the merchant will out-rival even honourable success in war, while they cannot but lessen the possibilities of international misunderstanding, and will draw closer the bonds of mutual respect and of our common brotherhood.

Thanking the Lord Mayor, 'the chief magistrate of the first city in the world', Ernest Forwood predicted that all businesses and trades would meet in the building, not only to do business but to exchange views on current questions of the day and to become 'knit together in friendly intercourse'. It was the greatest and most complete Exchange in the country, if not the whole world. It was no empty cliché for Ernest Forwood to say it was for him a proud and happy moment. For few can faith and dogged persistence have been crowned with such complete success. The Jeffrey's Square project was entirely his brain-child.

The last meeting of the Baltic Committee took place on 9 July 1903. The Baltic was dead, long live the Baltic!

THREE

TAKING NO TIME AT ALL

for fixing round the globe

Coming from the Shipping Exchange, James Findlay – the 'dictator' who ruled the Baltic Exchange at St Mary Axe – was naturally anxious to develop its maritime role, but was always open to any suggestion for expansion. He agreed to allow the Timber Trades Federation to join on equal terms with the original Baltic members in 1903, though he refused to admit members of the petroleum trade. He had honorary agents of the Exchange appointed in ports on various trade routes round the world and invited them to submit monthly reports. He supported the formation of the Baltic and White Sea Conference in 1905, designed to regulate freights and reconcile opposing interests of merchants and shipowners on such matters as the strike and ice clauses in charter-parties. He encouraged the formation of the London Cattle Food Trade Association in August 1906 to establish uniform contracts and arbitration systems for the cake and meal trade. He saw the goodwill which could come from the activities of the Baltic Amateur Dramatic and Orchestral Society formed in 1907 – which soon changed its name to the Baltic Amateur Dramatic and Operatic Society and presented straight and musical plays, mainly at the Scala Theatre in Charlotte Street. A member of the cast in their production of *The Rose of Persia* in 1910 was a clerk in the accounts department of shipbrokers Watts, Watts & Company called Ronald Colman, who became the well-known Hollywood film actor. The society brought the curtain down on its activities only with the demolition of the Scala Theatre in 1967.

Findlay acted as honorary secretary of the committee which was the precursor of the Institute of Shipbrokers, formed in 1911 after a deputation of shipbrokers told him of their wish to have an organisation to safeguard their interests and improve their status. The committee was

not formally associated until 1913, and in 1920 it obtained a royal charter as the Institute of Chartered Shipbrokers.

Shipping involved the world, and when the world went to war in August 1914 the Baltic found itself divided into warring camps corresponding to the belligerents in the field. When Britain declared war against Germany and her allies – which included Bulgaria, Austria and Turkey – the directors considered it their duty to distinguish not only the commercial sheep from the commercial goats but the King's friends from the King's enemies. On 12 August the directors resolved 'until further notice no German shall be allowed to enter the exchange', though that did not apply to any who were naturalised British subjects. After the sinking of the *Lusitania* in May 1915 they suspended all members, and their clerks, of German, Austrian and Turkish birth, even though they might be naturalised British subjects, and then decided to admit no one of eligible age who had not offered to join up.

The Baltic was still predominantly a grain exchange, and throughout the Great War the government allowed members to trade individually. There was a pooling system of ships, but not through the government. In 1916 the Trades Union Council asked Mr Asquith, the prime minister, to demand state ownership and control of all merchant shipping. The government would not hear of it, but by November 1918, when the war ended, a large state merchant fleet had come into being, including prize ships and vessels bought and registered in the name of the Controller of Shipping, who was a member of the Baltic.

It was difficult for most to forgive 'the enemy' for making such a havoc of their lives, and when victory came with the Armistice of 1918 and the following year the Treaty of Versailles spelled out the peace terms, few members were ready to forgive or forget. At the annual general meeting in June 1919 they altered their rules to admit only those who had been born in the British Empire before 31 December 1915.

Steamships and sailing ships lying in the harbour of Constantinople, waiting to be called up the narrow canal that connects the Bosphorus with the Black Sea, a trade with which so many Turkey merchants on the Baltic were concerned.

Members in khaki service dress and Sam Brown belts (right), on leave from the army, mingle with brokers and grain traders in City suits, bowler hats and toppers on the Floor at St Mary Axe in 1916 during the Great War.

The return to peacetime conditions was the moment for the directors of the Baltic, the clearing house for the cereal produce of a world that had stopped fighting, to overhaul the mechanics of the exercise and eliminate the evils which had developed during the conflict. To find an answer to the question 'Was a broker really necessary?' they called a series of conferences in 1927 with grain merchants, millers and seed crushers, and grain and oilseed brokers. Apart from giving their views on the role of

The Corn Exchange in Mark Lane during the early part of the twentieth century.

brokers, many expressed opinions on the Baltic's own role as the self-appointed regulator of the natural course of trade. Several criticised the Baltic's assumed right to impose unified procedures. How far could, or should, rules 'interfere' with free methods of buying and selling? How far was it desirable for the Baltic Exchange to become a brokers' protection society?

In the 1920s some 250,000 tons of grain were bought and sold on the Floor at St Mary Axe every day, worth about £2½ million. In spite of the attempts of big combines on the Continent and elsewhere to avoid the expense of a middleman, the use of Baltic brokers was increasing. During their attendance on the Floor each day they not only ascertained as early as possible what shippers were offering – the kinds of grain and the periods of shipment – but also a great deal of other valuable information to help them judge probable market fluctuations, with which to advise prospective buyers and sellers. A broker was able to get concessions on price and terms which neither buyer nor seller could manage if they met face to face. In the 1920s, in the course of a series of brief conversations on the Floor of the Baltic, a chartering clerk obtained a firm offer of a vessel, and a firm bid for the carriage of cargo by her, very much more easily and swiftly than was possible by telephone, telegram or letter.

The clerk had the satisfaction of knowing that he was working in the ship chartering centre of the world. London was not only the shipping but also the financial and insurance centre of all international trade. Shipbrokers on the Baltic represented shipowners based in Britain, and also overseas owners who had tramp tonnage to manage. The London market was so important that no foreign shipowner could afford to ignore it, or be without regular information about its activities.

At St Mary Axe the 'floor situation' of the Royal Exchange with its Walks was being repeated – daily intercourse between those with empty holds and those with cargoes to fill them, and the quick exchange of information and contracts on the basis of mutual trust and respect. The tightness of the St Mary Axe community, and the familiarity of members one with the other, had the effect of stabilising rates, ensuring that no shipowner needed to take any lower rate than his neighbour and – however far he was from London or from the ship he was going to charter – that no shipper of goods had need to fear he would have to pay anything more than the market rate of freight for his shipment.

The personal responsibilities of shipbrokers were considerable, and to insure them against any professional negligence in the course of their duties the Chartered Shipbrokers' Protection and Indemnity Association was formed in December 1925. In 1937 it was incorporated as the Chartered Shipbrokers' Protection Association Ltd.

By the end of the 1920s not only ships but also aeroplanes were being chartered to carry goods. In February 1929 S Instone & Company issued Britain's first air charter-party, an adaptation of a shipping charter-party. It was on behalf of a client who wished to send goods by an Imperial Airways flight from Croydon to Berlin. This was a welcome extension of the role of the broker, who in 1929 found his business somewhat reduced by the formation of the Millers Mutual, composed of large combines concentrating their buying of grain and dealing with merchants direct. To help bring back brokerage business in this field to the Baltic in March 1929, the London Corn Trade Association established a futures market at St Mary Axe in Canadian wheat on the lines of the one operated at South Sea House in 1897. For the purpose the LCTA created the London Grain Futures Association. A broker member of the Baltic who wished to join this had to sign the Exchange's 'Broker's Letter'. Introduced as far back as 1910, this stated that he was carrying on business solely as a broker or agent and would never deal on his own account. Shipbrokers signed a similar letter.

Calls on the skills of brokers fell away, however, as the world moved into the economic crises of the 1930s. The trade patterns altered by World War 1 returned for the most part to their normal channels in the 1920s, but with the demands made on them for post-war reconstruction at home, nations tended to give priority to protecting their own interests and giving employment to their own workforces. International considerations took second place. Emphasis on protectionism, self-sufficiency and national employment policies became more marked with world depression. The earnings of those engaged in the international sea-borne carrying trade slumped. By 1929 the number of people able to pay their 20-guinea annual subscription to the Baltic had fallen from the 2,770 of 1922 – and even the 2,377 of 1913 – to 2,368.

. The good news for those who did find the time and the money to use the Floor at St Mary Axe, in order to obtain the up-to-date information on which their business depended, was the merger in 1929 of Marconi's Wireless Telegraph Company and the Eastern Telegraph Company as Imperial and International Communications Ltd, soon changed to 'Cable

This massive machine, manufactured by Louis Schopper of Leipzig, was used to weigh samples. In 1994 it was still in the Baltic's damaged building at 14–20 St Mary Axe.

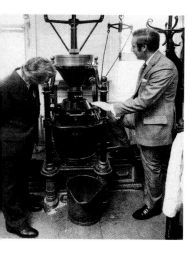

and Wireless'. Wireless was hardly a new medium of communication in 1929 – Marconi had opened a full transatlantic wireless telegraph service to America twenty years before, and in May 1924 he had spoken to Australia from England on a radio telephone. But the instantaneous transmission of information across the ether from hundreds of short-wave radio stations, with the degree of reliability now achieved, enabled the tramp shipping community to give charterers a service in which their customers, the buyers of their merchandise, would have confidence, and would be kept informed of changes in estimated times of arrival.

For the Baltic Mercantile & Shipping Exchange Ltd the falling off of members' subscription income was compensated for by what they received from office rents. The company paid a 12½ per cent dividend in 1929, and their £5 shares changed hands for £8. James Findlay wished the London County Council had allowed him to add another floor to Exchange Buildings in 1920, but that would have put them 3 feet above the permissible height of 80 feet.

Beautiful and intricate stained-glass windows, beneath a half dome, commemorated the Baltic dead of the Great War. Erected in 1922, the five windows of this striking memorial depict Truth, Justice, Fortitude, Faith, and Hope.

A pen-and-wash drawing by Geoffrey Fletcher, showing the rostrum from which the blue-uniformed waiters called the names of members.

With the onset of worsening world depression after 1929, fewer and fewer individuals and firms felt able to pay the subscription. In the year ending 31 March 1931, 296 resigned – though with some 168 joining, total membership only fell to 2,228. 'The figures for 1931', the chairman told shareholders at the next annual general meeting, 'were the lowest we have had for the past ten years, and I am sorry to say that this year's total is lower still.' 'Shipowner with 50 Years in Tramp Shipping' wrote to *Fairplay* in January 1932 to say that, though he had seen bad times and even very hopeless-looking times, he had never seen anything to compare with the year then closing. He said 1930 was bad, but 1931 had been worse. 'At the time that I write I should hope that the very worst depth of all has been reached.' It had not. According to the Tramp Shipping Administrative Committee's sixth report, the years 1930 to 1935 were the worst period ever experienced by British shipping. Between 1931 and 1933 some 3½ million gross tons of British shipping was laid up. Though in 1914 48 per cent of the world's merchant tonnage was British, in 1937 the figure had fallen to 32.5 per cent. British tanker fleet tonnage increased between the wars – it was 2.7 million in 1938 – but dry cargo tonnage declined.

At the luncheon to which the Baltic invited delegates of the World Monetary and Economic Conference held in London in 1933, Sir Herbert Robson, the chairman, told his guests:

> We who labour daily in this exchange live by international trade. Our business is connected with ships and the merchandise which moves in ships. The enormous decline in international trade has hit us harder than any section of the commercial community. It is we who have felt the full blast of the economic storm.

The free trade which the regulars at the Baltic Coffee House had celebrated with such ardour ninety years before, with the repeal of the Corn Laws, had vanished. British ships were largely idle because so many nations had seemed determined to limit international trade by enormous tariffs, and even by prohibition of imports except under a quota of negligible proportions.

> Our merchants are hampered at every turn because from hour to hour no man knows the value of the exchanges. Your business as delegates is to seek means of restoring international trade. If you fail there is a dark future before us all, not only on this exchange and in this country, but throughout every civilised country.

After thirty-three years as secretary, James Findlay retired in the spring of 1932. At a farewell meeting on the Floor, the chairman described him as 'the architect of our great institute'. He had prepared the plans, and the members had been the builders of what had the three-fold object of serving chartered shipbrokers, shipowners and merchants. Findlay gave the portrait painted by Maurice Codner – his parting present – to the Exchange. He was succeeded by his son Gilbert Findlay, who had been assistant secretary since June 1929.

When James Findlay died in 1935, the days of the Baltic Exchange as a commodity market were over. By the end of the decade, with the revival of shipping and the concentration of business into big combines such as ICI and Unilever, and with the great advances in telecommunications technology and the increasing size of tankers, the Baltic was changing from a commodity market into a freight market.

In 1938 the directors reported that the signs were that a point had been reached when improved conditions in trade could be expected to develop gradually. But it was the year of the Munich crisis, when the German Führer was proclaiming his plans for forcibly introducing a new order for Europe. The directors added to their forecast 'provided no international complications arise'.

James Arbuckle Findlay, the first secretary of the Baltic Mercantile & Shipping Exchange, who held the position for thirty-three years.

Apart from the possibility of so drastic a change of circumstances as would come from a second bout of German aggression in twenty years, the business scene at home – with the cost of maintaining an office in the City rising every year – was also changing. There were bigger rates, taxes and insurance premiums, higher wages for clerks and executives, and higher postal and telephone charges. There were fewer and fewer one-man and two-man partnerships of the kind that had constituted so large a part of the Baltic membership up to the mid-1930s. As millers amalgamated and shipping companies grouped, the hundred members on the Floor who had represented fifty firms in 1938 covered some five or six companies each with twenty or thirty representatives.

Between the wars membership of the Baltic was divided into 50 per cent shipping, and the other half grain (37 per cent) and oil seed (13 per cent). In 1938 a fourth division emerged, air freight. In April Captain Alfred Instone, who had pioneered airborne cargo in 1919, sounded out airline operators on the idea of setting up an air freight section on the Baltic. Gilbert Findlay organised a meeting at St Mary Axe of anyone interested in the idea, presided over by the chairman, Frank Fehr. Once Britain's armament requirements had been met, said Fehr, builders would concentrate on producing new kinds of civilian aircraft capable of carrying big loads over long distances. If the Baltic became the point where all business connected with air transport could be centralised, it would make for fair rates of freight, prevent unfair competition, provide a meeting place for plane builders and buyers, and be a means of ascertaining freight requirements. The shipbroker was not far away from the flying-ship broker. Just as they had the tramp ship, in the near future they would have the tramp aeroplane.

The meeting passed a resolution saying the time had arrived to open membership of the Exchange to those engaged in air transport. Alfred Instone hoped the time for forming an air freight section was opportune. But, of course, it was not. Come 3 September 1939 the world would once again be engaged in armed conflict. Overnight it halted the recovery which was just gathering momentum, stifled promising ideas such as a

Baltic air freight market and killed off the short lives of the Manitoba Wheat and La Plata Maize Futures Markets instigated in 1933.

For a long time now, brokers on the Baltic, the international chartering centre, had ceased to depend solely on the British merchant navy for their business. They 'fixed' cargoes for ships of all nationalities, and from ports in one part of the world to another without touching the British Isles. The whole of the world's shipping was their business. But from 3 September 1939 the world became divided into three: Britain and her allies, the enemy and the neutrals. The size and carrying power of the British mercantile marine, and in particular the tramp shipping part of it, immediately reassumed special significance. It was still by far the largest in the world, but in 1939 44 per cent by weight of the commodities imported into the UK came in foreign ships. How far the allied and neutral shipowning countries of Europe would help Britain out was unknown. There was no parallel for shipping resembling the Food (Defence Plans) Department of the Board of Trade which had been preparing for a war situation since 1936. The Committee of Imperial Defence did not consider shipping requirements until the Munich crisis of 1938. It was reckoned that British tonnage would be able to import about 48 million tons of dry cargo in the first twelve months of the war, sufficient for all needs. Plans to regulate merchant shipping were considered, but shelved in 1938. The government first favoured a licensing system to control freight rates and run the country's merchant shipping through the trade, as it was doing with food. But on 13 October they set up what members of the Baltic most feared, a Ministry of Shipping, with Sir John Gilmour as minister, just when the Baltic was busy forming committees to organise the chartering of vessels on behalf of the Board of Trade. There were to be chartering committees for each geographical market. Frank Alexander, the chairman of the Baltic, had already made considerable progress with the Treasury over the amount of commission to be paid to the chartering pool on all Ministry of Food charters. After a few weeks of war, however, the country began to run short of wheat; imports in September and October 1939 were only about half consumption. On 4 January 1940, therefore, the government decided to abandon the licensing system and to introduce direct requisition of ships.

Gilbert Findlay, assistant secretary from 1929, who succeeded his father and was secretary for twenty-two years, from 1932 to 1954.

Five days after their announcement, Frank Alexander wrote to the government pointing out that, as an institution, the Baltic was a vital pillar of the economic system, and that the profession of broker and chartering agent should be preserved as far as possible during the time of war, so that at the end of hostilities they might be in a position to resume their normal trading. *Fairplay* agreed: 'In the event of the requisitioning of British tonnage lock, stock and barrel becoming the order of the day then the very lifeblood of British tramp owners as represented by the freight market must in consequence stagnate to no inconsiderable degree.'

It was the policy of the government that British shipowners should not be allowed to amass large profits out of the emergency of the state. However, it was not possible, said *Fairplay*, to contemplate with any degree of equanimity the wiping out of so essential a service to the nation, much in the manner of a gentleman with a duster.

Sir John Gilmour defended his policy by denying that any ship the government requisitioned was taken from the experienced hands of the owners and delivered to the mercies of a body of civil servants. They did not in fact even hand the ships over to the shipowners or the ministry. They took the ship over as a running concern. The owners remained, continuing to operate it as though upon their own business. The ministry would instruct them from time to time, as required, to carry certain cargoes and to follow certain routes, and in such matters they had the advantage of expert shipowners to advise them. Chartering was on a time basis.

Members of the Baltic assembled at St Mary Axe at the beginning of March 1940 to pass a resolution protesting at the displacement by the Ministry of Shipping of the chartering committees, and at the creation of the ministry's City Central Chartering Office – which they considered detrimental to the national interest. They placed on record the intense disappointment felt at the failure of the ministry to remedy the serious hardship and loss of livelihood imposed upon shipbrokers and chartering agents by control and chartering of tonnage. It was a resolution of the meeting, not of the board of the Baltic Exchange. Whatever the government decided to do, said Frank Alexander who took the chair, the Baltic would retain their freedom to endorse or oppose and criticise. They were putting national interest in the foreground, and their own interests and personal considerations second. In a speech to shareholders at their annual general meeting a couple of months later, by which time Winston Churchill had replaced Neville Chamberlain as prime minister, he again emphasised the need to preserve members' skills for when conditions returned to normal.

The outstanding position of London and of Britain in the whole of the commercial world, he said, was mainly due to the activities and enterprise shown by brokers and middlemen, combined with the high standard of moral integrity which stood out pre-eminently; and it had always been the aim of the board to watch jealously to ensure that that high standard was maintained unimpaired:

> This is shown by the fact that throughout the world membership of the Baltic Exchange is looked upon as a hallmark of integrity. The merchant princes and shipping magnates may with a great deal of truth be said to have built up their businesses on the activities of the middlemen and brokers who in their incessant search to make commissions for themselves investigate and recommend fresh avenues of enterprise and commerce to their principals. In all our negotiations with the Government we have stressed the importance and value of keeping the middlemen and brokers commercially as well as financially alive even in time of war when perhaps their usefulness is not so obvious, so that they may be able to resume their normal functions in happier days ... The middleman and the broker will never be eliminated provided they render useful service in which they become the creators of business and not in any sense parasites on it.

It was putting a brave face on a situation, the more brutal reality of which was expressed in two sentences in the directors' report of 7 May 1940: 'The outbreak of war last September and the action of the Government in immediately taking over control of all imports into this country, together with control of shipping, has completely altered the

Sunlight filters through the huge glass domes above the Exchange Floor (right) as merchants and brokers start the morning session in the 1950s. The busts of John Walker (right) and Edward Pembroke (left) (see page 68) may be seen on either side of the marble fireplace.

business hitherto conducted in the Exchange. Many members have been faced with almost complete loss of their business and income.'

For better or worse the Baltic Exchange suspended its operations 'for the duration'. It became, in the words of the London *Evening Standard*, the City's 'Ghost Exchange'.

> Once the hub of the world of commerce, it is now almost deserted. ... The days when it was a hive of activity and echoed to bids of merchants and brokers are gone. Now it echoes only to the ghostlike footfalls of the few members who use 'the floor' of the Exchange chiefly out of personal habits. Pre-war footfalls would not have been heard above the buzz of business. Now scarcely any business is transacted.

From four to six o'clock each afternoon the Floor echoed to the drill routines of young members of the City of London Air Training Corps hoping to join the Royal Air Force. Fire watchers witnessed a direct hit on No. 14 St Mary Axe next door in April 1941, which damaged the Exchange to some extent. Incendiary bombs fell on the fourth floor in December. A shrewd member bought the bombed site of No. 14 from the Duchy of Lancaster as a possible post-war extension. Water from the artesian well on the Floor was 'lent' to the London Fire Brigade to help them fight the fires lit by the Luftwaffe's merciless *Blitzkrieg*. Some £8,500 was raised to present three Spitfire fighter planes to the RAF; these were called 'Baltic Exchange 1', '2' and '3'. By November 1941 the Baltic had given the government £447,870 as a free-of-interest loan.

Though there was no longer a role for the Baltic as there had been in peacetime, the government relied on their most experienced members to help organise carrying to a beleaguered Britain the vital food and other supplies in the very different circumstances of total war.

Fred Leathers, a director of William Cory, coal importers, and a leading member of the Baltic, was an old friend of Winston Churchill, in whose constituency he lived. When Churchill became prime minister in May 1940 he invited him to put his very considerable knowledge of shipping at the disposal of the government. The prime minister made him a member of the House of Lords and head of the new Ministry of War Transport, a merger of the Ministries of Shipping and of Transport. The Ship Management Division of the new ministry dealt directly, and through owners, with the employment of deep-sea tramps and chartered and seized foreign vessels, and purchased newly built vessels. It also controlled the City Central Chartering Office. Its Shipping (Operations) Control was under the chairmanship of Sir Vernon Thomson of Union Castle, a past chairman of the Baltic, who undertook close supervision of shipping under Viscount Leathers. Sir Gibson Graham, another leading Baltic figure (who became chairman in 1953) was deputy director of commercial services at the Ministry of War Transport and represented the ministry in the Mediterranean.

The grain trade had maintained contact with the government throughout the inter-war period through the National Federation of Corn Trade Associations, which had been created for this purpose in 1919 and never disbanded. Planning for food control in the event of another war had been begun by the Food (Defence Plans) Department of the Board of Trade in 1936. When war broke out three years later J V Rank was appointed chairman of the Imported Cereals Committee of the Cereals Control Board of the Ministry of Food, which put into operation well-formulated plans for smooth transition into control through the trade. The committee organised the buying of foreign grain through shippers, and its distribution through merchants with the aid of brokers. The expertise of the trade was harnessed through the Port Area Grain Committees and the National Federation of Corn Trade Associations. As president of the NFCTA, Baltic member Sir Leslie Phillips was responsible at the Ministry of Food for the food shipping programme and the food warehousing programme.

Sir Frank Alexander, chairman of the Exchange 1939–45 and Lord Mayor of London 1944–5. Sir Frank's son, Sir Charles Gundry Alexander, was a director of the Exchange from 1964 to 1968.

It was Baltic members who made all this work smoothly by being allowed to continue to practise their trade in the various port organisations and on the staffs of the government bodies concerned.

Frank Alexander, knighted in the New Year Honours of 1942, was elected Lord Mayor of London in 1944. Though two members of the Baltic, Sir Charles Batho (1927) and Sir Charles Trinder (1968) were Lord Mayor before and after this, Sir Frank Alexander was the first chairman of the Exchange to hold that distinguished office. And he did so exactly two hundred years after Reynallds and Winboult refashioned their commercial resort in Threadneedle Street as the Virginia and Baltick Coffee House. In 1744 those operating Britain's sea-borne carrying trade had a hard struggle to keep the supply lines open in the face of French and Spanish aggression. The year 1944 found Britain in the same situation, battling this time against a German Reich intent, in league with its axis partner Japan, on making the world submit to the unacceptable ideas of government which it called national socialism. In 1944, however, there was no longer any fear that the evil partners would succeed. As A J P Taylor has written, by the end of 1944 nearly all the conquests made by Germany and Japan had been lost, and the homelands of the conquerors were themselves threatened: 'Though 1944 did not see final Allied victory, it was for many, especially in western Europe, the year of liberation.'

The assumption was that it was only a matter of months before Germany surrendered and Britain returned – though only gradually – to conditions resembling those of times which for the second time people looked back upon nostalgically as 'Before the War'. In August 1944 the government issued a White Paper setting out the plans of the United Maritime Authority to continue co-ordinated control of all merchant shipping resources of the victorious allies now grouped politically as the United Nations. One of its two secretariats was established in London by the Ministry of War Transport. Its planning committee drew up procedures

The Baltic serves not only shipbrokers but those engaged in the international air-borne carrying trade – a mobile crane being loaded at London airport on to a Russian cargo aircraft.

for programming and allocating dry cargo and tanker tonnage, and the settling of freight rates. A few weeks before the European war ended in May 1945, representatives of thirty-eight firms met at the Baltic and formed a pool for French chartering business, encouraged by the ministry's agreement to recognise the use of chartering agents. Furness Withy urged the formation of a Russian chartering pool on the same lines. When Lord Leathers let it be known that he looked forward to the re-establishment of the UK chartering markets as an important factor in the revival of British overseas trade, the Institute of Chartered Shipbrokers presented him with a document giving their views on how best to return to normal practices. Leathers told them that he would be prepared for brokers to participate as soon as possible in fixtures for ministry-controlled deep-sea tramp vessels in certain additional export and cross trades with a maximum commission of £75, which would treble their number of fixtures.

Sir Frank Alexander arranged for freight requirements of the Ministry of Food to be undertaken by chartering agents who were members of the Baltic. He told the ministry that the system of having a large number of specialised freight committees, of the kind created in the early days of the war, was no longer practicable. Instead he proposed a small main committee of five members of the Baltic, experienced in chartering grain, rice, sugar, oil, oilseeds and so on, to meet under the chairmanship of Henry Brewer, vice-chairman of the Exchange, and to organise all the Ministry of Food's freight.

Persistent lobbying of the Ministry of War Transport by the General Council of British Shipping resulted in their issuing in September 1945 an announcement headed 'Restoration of Chartering Machinery'. It mainly concerned deep-sea tramp shipping. The ministry proposed introducing a modified system of procedure for the allocation of vessels 'designed as a preliminary stage in the restoration of the ordinary commercial machinery for the chartering of tonnage'. By this the ministry retained full control of the direction of voyages, but shipowners and their brokers could arrange chartering and conclude fixtures without altering their responsibilities or the ministry's. Brokerages were allowed when tramp ships were employed and voyage charters were signed for the carriage of imports to Britain, but there would be a limitation of £100. 'The Ministry of War Transport', ran the council's announcement, 'are taking steps to bring these proposals to the attention of the Baltic Exchange and to consult them as necessary, with a view to facilitating the smooth working of the scheme.'

The Baltic was back in business.

By VE Day in May 1945 its membership had fallen to 1,287. Subscription and entrance fees amounted to only £21,600, but income from rents were more than double that, at £44,000. After seven years the Exchange was solvent, and ended the war with a balance of £1,890, having received £480,299 and paid out £478,409. The company also had £16,000 in reserve and a sum of £800 for building contingencies.

Chairmen of the Baltic traditionally held office for two years, but Sir Frank Alexander stayed in the chair throughout the six war years. In his last address as chairman to shareholders at the 1946 annual general meeting he reiterated that their international business was largely dependent on the maintenance of free markets, and that these could not exist if the governments in consumer or producer countries decided to continue bulk buying or selling. He recognised that control of foodstuffs and many essential commodities had to continue during the period of shortage and readjustment, but he hoped they would be relaxed at the earliest possible moment: 'I hope too that it will be admitted that the prestige of the Baltic stands higher today than ever before, and that we have established a reputation for service to our country and to international trade based on the highest standard of upright dealing without undue regard to our own personal advantage.'

There was no question of returning to the world of before the war. However, Alfred Instone's project to form an air freight section was revived, and the Airbrokers Association came into being in 1949. The Baltic became the world's first air freight exchange. This grew out of the Air Freight Advisory Committee which came into being in March 1948 with W Stanley Hinde as chairman. The directors of the Baltic were not able to give them the premises at St Mary Axe for which they asked, and they acquired rent-free accommodation in the offices of the Institute of Chartered Shipbrokers. They drafted air charter-parties in conjunction with the British Air Charter Association, which had been formed in July 1949 – 'Baltaircon' for consecutive flights, 'Baltairvoy' for air voyage cargo, with the 'Baltairnote' consignment note. That year the Advisory Committee became the Airbrokers Association with Jack Logan as full-time secretary; he was made a member of the Exchange and the new association's representative. Wings were incorporated in the Baltic's coat-of-arms, and an international air market took the floor at St Mary Axe alongside the old shipping market. Richard Hyde, a barrister who in 1933 had joined shipbrokers J E Hyde founded by his father in 1908, drafted the clauses of a revised 'Baltairvoy', and reworded the 'Baltairpac' and 'Balticheck'. An air arbitration panel was formed.

Although during the thirteen years in which the Ministry of Food was Britain's only purchaser the grain section of the Baltic was dormant, it was only a matter of waiting for it to return, in whatever form post-war circumstances might dictate.

The first stage in decontrol did not come until 1952. Sir Leslie Phillips and other members of the Baltic helped the Federation of Corn Trade Associations with the smooth release of the ministry's stocks. But there were few successors to the large number of commodity brokers who had daily filled the Bury Street end of the Floor in the 1920s and 1930s. Amalgamations and improved communications had reduced the need for their presence. A Commonwealth radio telephone system went into operation in March 1949 at the arbitrary charge of £1 a minute, very much less than the only other radio telephone service of the day across the Atlantic that cost five times as much. One of the pioneers of radio telephony was J H 'Tug' Wilson, who had been one of the five 'Via Imperial' messenger boys on call in the tiny room behind the public counter of the old telegraph office at the Baltic.

The crowd of commodity brokers was replaced by a few men trading on behalf of the large companies who, nevertheless, in due course handled larger quantities of grain and other commodities than the many had handled pre-war.

Membership soon began to rise as shipbrokers and clerks returned from the services and government offices. On the advice of the Building Committee appointed in 1947 to consider post-war expansion, the Exchange company bought the bombed site at 14–20 St Mary Axe. They were not however granted a licence to build on it the planned annexe to house the secretariat, and offices to let to tenants, until 1953. Making the arrangements for this extension was the last major task of the much liked and highly efficient Gilbert Findlay, who retired as secretary and manager in 1954 after twenty-two years. He was succeeded by Jack Walker, who had been on the administrative staff for the previous thirty-seven years.

Sir Winston Churchill laid the foundation stone of the new building on 2 March 1955 – the last he laid as prime minister. He brought his union card with him to show his qualification for the job. At an evening ceremony on 21 November 1956, Queen Elizabeth II formally opened the extension and named, as the Queen's Room, the large banqueting hall in the basement. At the same time the Floor was relaid with Rhodesian teak blocks and much of the underpinning was strengthened. The rebirth of the Baltic Exchange was also marked by the adoption of a new coat-of-arms based on that of the South Sea Company.

What needed refurbishing more than anything else was the rule book. Failure to enlist the help of a lawyer to amend the rules and articles had landed the old Baltic Committee in many scrapes. An urge to tinker with the guidelines, to refine and adjust, had led to a mass of verbiage which exasperated more than one solicitor whom the committee had reluctantly agreed to consult. Viewing the tangle which they had inherited, Baltic members of the 1960s decided that the time had come for a penetrating, commonsense rethink of the rules in line with current circumstances, to make them more comprehensible to those whom they were designed to guide. In submitting their recommendations to an extraordinary general meeting in June 1966, the sub-committee, led by Richard Hyde, which

Prime Minister Sir Winston Churchill, with his inevitable cigar, chats with Mrs Gibson-Graham, the chairman's wife, and the Archbishop of Canterbury at lunch after Sir Winston had laid the foundation stone of Baltic Exchange Chambers, 14–20 St Mary Axe.

volunteered to undertake the task of giving fresh life to the original principles, hoped that they were sufficiently embracing to avoid further alterations for some years to come.

Up to 1966 a woman could have been elected a member of the Exchange if the board had been so inclined, since the rule on candidates only referred to 'a person' and 'a British subject' without specifying the gender. The new Rule 4 of 1966 stipulated that a member or principal must be 'any male British subject or Commonwealth citizen or citizen of the Republic of Eire over 21 years' or 'any male foreign subject'. So, from then on women were excluded not by the discretion of the board but by the rule book. After the Exchange's solicitor had vetted the sub-committee's proposals, the meeting, presided over by the chairman, Lord Kilmarnock, accepted them in their entirety.

Most of the members of the Baltic were shipbrokers, and the great majority were members of their own institute. By the 1970s shipbroking had become a very much more homogeneous activity than ten years before, though there was still a clear distinction between shipbrokers and sale and purchase (S&P) brokers.

The sale and purchase of ships by public auction under the hammer at St Mary Axe hardly survived World War 2. The first public auction of a ship in the UK for twenty-five years took place at the Baltic in March 1982 – it was the first there in living memory. The ship was the 6,342-ton roll-on roll-off vessel *Butterfly*, on bareboat charter to an Italian shipping group who had run out of cash and had fourteen other ships impounded by creditors. The contract the Italians had with the Singapore owners stipulated that in case of default the vessel must be sold by public auction.

The days when Mr Harland – before he teamed up with Mr Wolff – had lunch at the Baltic every day and sat in the Room in his top hat discussing orders for his Belfast yard were long past. New ships were made to order; old ships changed hands by private treaty through brokers such as Kellocks and Eggar Forrester, who had a special ship sale, purchase and construction division. But the huge cost of a ship involved a would-be purchaser in complicated arrangements with banks, and chartering became a more profitable exercise than owning. There were sale and purchase brokers on the floor of the Baltic Exchange every day in 1974, however, and they were there to do business.

There were no longer divisions in the shipping side. There were no longer specialists in particular commodities or in the trade of a particular part of the world. A broker on the Baltic specialised in the world – in dry cargo as well as oil, in charter-parties for grain as well as phosphates, in time and voyage charters, in the maritime laws of Bolivia as well as France, in the docking facilities of Gdansk as well as of Alexandria, the demurrage rates at Rotterdam, the trimming charges at Karachi, the discharging facilities required for steel coils and bundled timber as well as bulk flour and bags of cement, insurance for the ice-bound Baltic Sea as well as the tropical Azores.

He knew the currency arrangements of Yugoslavia; the fuelling facilities on the China coast; the cubic feet taken by a ton of pumice; whether five days was a reasonable time for loading twenty thousand tons of zinc concentrates; the price of produce in Nigeria, Norway and New Zealand, where it originated and the price it would attain in Britain, Mexico and Italy where it was consumed. He acquainted himself with the complicated exchange control requirements and the Bank of England forms for transferring currency. His knowledge might be nothing less than encyclopaedic – and without the aid of a personal computer. He had to carry the information in his head. Moreover, he had to rely on experience to interpret inflections of broken English on a bad line from Bremen, so that he was able quickly to conclude that it was the panicky Rheinlander's radar that was damaged, not his rudder, and that his intended departure in spite of this mishap was not so hazardous as it first sounded.

The superintendent of the Floor, Arthur Bone (right), inspects his blue-jacketed, yellow-collared and top-hatted 'waiters' prior to the Exchange opening for business. Shown left to right are Fred Veryard, George Hart and Fred Codrai.

A typical firm of the 1970s probably had exclusive representation of one British shipowner, and at the same time acted for several foreign and British shipowners, each of whom employed a number of shipbrokers both in Britain and abroad. It represented not only shipowners seeking a customer to charter their ships but manufacturers and merchants – shippers/charterers – seeking a ship to carry their goods. It also acted for other shipbrokers in different parts of the world. Simultaneous searching took place in every direction for the world's freight requirements every hour of every day and every night. In June 1972, however, tonnage of the world's merchant fleet laid up through lack of work was at the highest level for ten years; 2 per cent of it was idle, amounting to 4,950,000 tons gross. As reported in *The Times*, 'the present recession has certainly lasted longer than most observers anticipated and coincided with a huge increase in costs'.

Unless they took a firm grip on their procedures, brokers' costs also mounted. Time was the vital factor in providing a service economically. Unless a broker had six private teleprinter lines connecting his office with six other offices over which he could send his message simultaneously, he could only put his enquiries out in order, ending with the sixth maybe half an hour or an hour later than the first. By the time the sixth received the question, the first might already have come up with an answer. Long-distance public telephone calls over post office lines took time in the 1970s, and money. A teleprinter message on the public international Telex network was only instantaneous once the machines at either end were connected via the various exchanges, and this took time and even more money. But unlike when he used the telephone, at least the originator had a written copy of his message, so there could be no dispute about what had been said; and there could be no question of waiting for the man at the receiving end to answer and agree to take the call, as happened before there was direct dialling. His teleprinter started printing out the message whether he was there or not.

Derek Prentis was one of the many who regarded the advent of Telex as a godsend. Learning the business with William H Muller & Company after being demobbed from the RAF in 1946, he had a stint as a coasting broker with Herbert Smart & Company and then moved to Moxey, Savon & Company who were engaged in owners' broking, chartering, merchanting, agency and insurance and operated as out-traders also. During his forty-six years in the shipping industry he has twice served as a director of the Baltic and has been chairman and president of the Institute of Chartered Shipbrokers. 'Telex was a godsend because in those days we used to have to code-up messages by learning the abbreviations to save money.' Everything took rather longer when he first came on the Floor in 1952. Working from 8.30 in the morning to 8.30 at night was not uncommon.

> It was more stringent in those days, just after the war. Some of the traditions still lingered. You could not walk up and address a Senior but had to speak to his clerk. Consequently, sometimes you would arrange a deal and your senior – the managing director or manager – would tie it up until you had learnt the trade. It was no good saying to your principal that you did not know what you were doing. You had to learn not only from his requirements regarding chartering, but also the ship itself. (*The Baltic*, Autumn 1992)

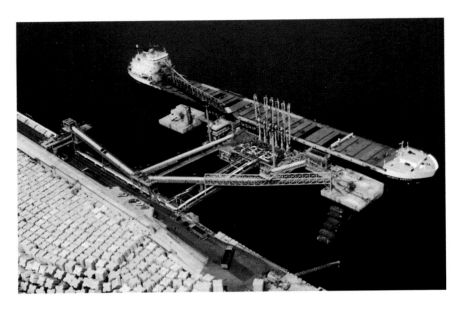

A self-discharging bulk carrier working at a temporary terminal.

To reduce the uncertainties of voyage charters, many shipowners looked to giving themselves a trouble-free income for months or maybe years on end by hiring their ships out on time-charter. Others spread the risks and shared the mounting costs by forming a consortium on the lines of Seabridge, who set up a broking panel to secure business. New ways of stowing, loading and discharging cargo were devised to reduce costs and save time — containerisation; unitisation; pallets; roll-on roll-off; bulk carriers of 150,000 tonnes and more; oil tankers of 200,000, 300,000 and even 500,000 tonnes deadweight — these were the very large crude carriers (VLCCs) and the ultra large crude carriers (ULCCs); chemical carriers; oil rig supply ships; composite ships for carriage of cars and bulk cargoes. All were capable of tramping or could be chartered for a period or a single voyage. Knowing their capabilities added to the volume and variety of knowledge with which the 1974 Baltic broker had to familiarise himself.

Containers stacked for loading by huge straddle cranes on the dockside.

PART II

POINT OF
REFERENCE
FOR THE WORLD

FOUR

NO EFFECTIVE SUBSTITUTE

for an international freight market in London

The smooth running of the Baltic Exchange, on which brokers and others depended to so large an extent for the efficient and economic conduct of their business, was due in no small way to the service on which they knew they could rely when, not so often as their predecessors, they went on the Floor. This derived from the accumulation of experience by long-serving staff such as Claude Mathers, who retired in 1971 after fifty years at St Mary Axe. Joining as a 15-year-old messenger boy in 1921, he succeeded C J Harrison as superintendent of the Baltic Exchange in 1965, and in his turn was succeeded by Arthur Kirby who had been with the Baltic for forty-two years.

They had served through great changes. Up to the 1930s the heads of all the firms, big and small, themselves walked the Floor every day and stayed for lunch. There was a queue for the telephones in those days and, without the aid of electronic public address equipment, the caller had difficulty in making his voice heard on the megaphone through the din of business chatter or James Findlay shouting to members to put their cigarettes out. Between the wars there was a bustle and an intensity which the 1974 scene lacked, though the setting was virtually the same.

The granite entrance up the steps from St Mary Axe led to the marble lobby with its stained-glass crests of Plymouth, Hull, Liverpool and other principal 'outports', of the Straits Settlements and other colonial territories whose names and allegiances had long changed. On the left stood the reminder of the no smoking rule, the binnacle of burnished brass made by Kelvin, Bottomley & Baird, demoted to an ash tray for the cigarette stubs of members, who were not allowed to take them on the Floor. The plaque giving the name of the vessel which it once guided had been so ardently polished that no trace of the words remained. On the right hung an *aide-mémoire* of what was *de rigueur* sartorially, reading: 'The attention of members is drawn to the fact that guests are expected to wear a lounge suit or its equivalent as this is the customary standard of dress for

Bibby Line's 28,000 cubic metre gas carrier, the Cheshire (left). *Highly specialised ships such as this operate in niche markets.*

members.' Visitors who came as guests could pass no further than this lobby until signed for and taken onto the Floor by their member host.

Off the lobby was the high-ceilinged room from which James Findlay had once kept a tight rein on happenings on the other side of the glass doors. This became an arbitration room, but in the 1950s it was redecorated as a VIP reception room and hung with a portrait of HRH The Duke of Edinburgh (elected as an honorary member in 1953).

The Floor of 1974 was the one opened by the Lord Mayor of London seventy years before. Its marble pillars were those round which the members of the 1930s used to roll their half-crowns, and those James Findlay reprimanded members for leaning against. Its red floor, onto which wet umbrellas seemed to drip blood, was not the floor of 1903; it was one which had replaced the original in 1956. The fine marble fireplaces no longer glowed with live coal fires. The siting of the marble rostrum, from which members' names were called, was now central, and above it hung a bell from the battleship HMS *Queen Elizabeth*, presented to the Exchange by Admiral Sir John Cunningham in 1958 for ringing on special occasions. A ring on an older bell, marked 'Ceres 1729', opened and closed daily sessions. This bell hung above the elevated desk of the Exchange superintendent, distinguished by his blue morning coat from the other fifteen uniformed and top-hatted Floor staff.

The bust of John Walker,[1] who died in 1854, still looked down on the members of 1974, as did the bearded bow-tied head of Edward Pembroke, 1831–1911, who was a member for fifty-seven years. At one end of the Room was an old Marratt barometer, and at the other end was a Royal Polytechnic barometer of 1869 made by Joseph Davis bearing 'Admiral Fitzroy's Special Remarks' on what to expect when rising and when falling.

These were relics of the days when the business done on the Baltic was greatly affected by the weather. Over one fireplace there had once been a 6-foot wind dial connected to a vane on the roof. It bore the points of the compass and a revolving finger which indicated the way the wind was blowing. It may have been the dial at South Sea House mentioned in the catalogue of sale; if so, no bids were made for it. Alfred Bunker, who first came on the Floor in 1919, remembered shipbrokers chortling when the arrow pointed to the south, which meant a quick passage up the Channel, and cursing when it pointed north, which boded a fortnight's delay. Sailing ships played a role to the end of the 1930s. For certain cargoes, such as nitrate from Chile, guano from Peru, soft timber from St John and Halifax, and grain from Australia, sailing ships continued to be the most suitable carriers. A sailing ship took three months from Australia against a steamer's fifty days, but for many commodities this was an advantage. When the commodity market was bad, the sailing ship could be used as a floating warehouse and discharge could be delayed to give the merchant elbow room to hedge. Old Mr McDougall used to charter two or three sailing ships a year right up to 1939.

Once a year, for the Armistice Day service, the hubbub of fixing ships

---

1 In 1923 the bust was found in the Post Office built on the site of the coffee house at 58 Threadneedle Street, and it was presented to the Baltic Exchange in that year.

gave way to the clamour of a military band marching and counter-marching up and down the Floor. It was one of the two regular occasions when women were allowed onto the Floor, and then they had to be out by noon. The other occasion was every other year, to attend with their husbands the cocktail party which the Baltic gave its retiring chairman to mark the end of his term of office.

Though the activity on the Floor on working days was frenzied, the process by which a member made contact with a distant client was somewhat ponderous. Putting through an overseas telephone call entailed filling in a 'trunk slip', giving it to the 'waiter' on the large dais against the wall and waiting for one's name to be called from the rostrum. A waiter on the dais could also call the attention of a member anywhere in the Exchange by dialling the number of the Teletracer which the member carried in his breast pocket. He collected it from the lobby when he entered. This miniature radio receiver picked up, from the aerial round the floor, the short-wave signal transmitted on the frequency to which it was tuned. It took the form of a 'bleep'. Members hired these new

The Exchange's caller, Stan Francis, at the rostrum, using the new public address system which carried announcements throughout the restaurants and bars as well as the Floor. Some announcements concerned telephone calls; a member who had filled in a 'trunk slip' for a long-distance call had to wait for the connection to be made.

pocket paging devices for an annual rent of £21. It was a far cry from the pre-war system when the waiter shouted 'Table!' and a page boy collected the telegram from the rostrum before pacing the Exchange to find the member it was for.

There was no Telex line to the Exchange in 1974, only two teleprinters giving commercial information, Stock Exchange prices and the Exchange Telegraph financial service. Other information was posted in sheets, as it had been for 150 years, on the Floor's notice boards. There was a reminder that there was no smoking in the dining room before two o'clock in the afternoon, and that only one guest was allowed in the main dining room at lunch. There was a notice telling members that in the secretary's room was a list of the companies and individuals who since 1961 had failed to honour arbitration awards, which any of them was at liberty to inspect. There was an invitation to send the chairman or secretary any information a member might have that was deemed likely to affect the eligibility of those applying for membership.

Richard Hyde's hopes that his new set of rules would last for some years were justified. There were no changes until May 1971, when the qualifications for eligible candidates were drastically redrafted. A stipulation was added that a company seeking membership must satisfy the board that it had a reasonably large capital – a minimum of £5,000 if the shareholders were in Britain, more if they were abroad. Most of the members were corporations – limited companies – in 1974. The individuals who had the right of entrée to the Exchange were the principals whom these companies nominated to represent them on the Floor. Representative principals and their clerks, as well as their companies, were personally elected by ballot of the fifteen directors of the Exchange, three of whom were 'ballot' directors (elected by a ballot of one-vote one-member) and the other twelve elected by shareholders whose voting power was determined by their shareholding. They were divided into shipping directors and commodity directors (renamed mercantile directors in 1973), and from 1971 there was also an air director. Companies such as the British Steel Corporation and Unilever, which represented a raw material user interest, were becoming members in increasing numbers.

For the chairman, elected in May or June for a term of two years, the duties were arduous. He presided over board meetings once a fortnight. He also often chaired *ad hoc* committees. He and his fellow directors were concerned not merely with running a business centre/market place/club, but with directing a highly successful property company and with striking a balance between the demands of all of these.

The chairman's position made him an *ex-officio* member of bodies such as the London Chamber of Commerce, the board of management of the Royal National Lifeboat Institution, and the City Liaison Committee of the National Economic Development Council. In 1971 Brian Turner, as chairman of the Baltic, made a first official overseas visit, to Australia.

The chairman was host whenever the Baltic entertained, a highlight being the annual Lord Mayor's luncheon, which had been a feature of the social year since the opening of St Mary Axe in 1903 and from 1957 was held in the Queen's Room. He attended a large number of City dinners and receptions, and appeared at the social and sporting functions of the Baltic's own clubs and societies – the bridge, soccer, cricket, hockey, rugger, rifle, squash and swimming clubs; the golfing and tennis societies; and the sailing association. The one-time boxing club and motor club had fallen by the way, and the Baltic Amateur Dramatic and Operatic Society held its last show in 1967.

The most taxing of his duties was resolving the variety of human problems with which he was inevitably confronted in the course of his term of office. Who was a suitable person to be a member of the Baltic and who was not? Armed with the report of the secretary at the preliminary interview, he conferred with his fellow directors on the written applications of each candidate. If, after discussion, he agreed with his colleagues that a candidate was unsuitable, and was unlikely to avoid being blackballed when it came to the directors' balloting, he told him so. This gave the candidate a chance to withdraw his application before his name was posted on the Floor as a candidate, the risk being that his name would not reappear a fortnight later as an elected member. The chairman, needless to say, would only try to persuade an unsuitable candidate to withdraw his application, to save him the probable public shame of being blackballed. The candidate could, of course, decline, and could take the risk of his name going to ballot and having to face the consequences of publicly known exclusion. He could have his name proposed the following year if he wished.

Even more demanding was dealing with complaints about the alleged ill-conduct of fellow members. Rule 30 stated that all complaints made by a member company or individual against another member had to be made in writing to the chairman, 'who may cause a copy thereof to be sent to the party against whom the complaint shall have been made'. If the chairman considered there was a *prima-facie* case for investigation, he would impanel three or four directors to interview both parties and examine their documents. However if, on the grounds of natural justice, he considered there was no occasion for taking action, he would tell the complainant, who could only accept the chairman's decision as final. If this small committee of directors considered the person complained about had done nothing to make him a potential offender under the rule about detrimental or unbecoming conduct, the complainant was so informed and there the matter had to rest. If they thought otherwise the case was referred to the whole board, who would decide whether to take disciplinary action by imposing censures, suspension or expulsion. A similar procedure was carried out when a non-member complained about a member.

For the most part, when the directors were called upon to consider a complaint, it was by a member about a non-member, probably an overseas operator about whose activities it was felt members in general should be warned. And the sooner the better. An outsider was unlikely to be willing to appear before a 'tribunal' without legal powers, which he did not recognise as having a right to call him before them, let alone to pronounce on the ethics of his conduct. All the directors could do was to instruct the secretary to place a notice on the Floor telling members that information was available about X, and saying that any member who went to the secretary's office would be told what he knew of X or be put in touch with the original informant. The notice was privileged – 'For Members Only' – and in any event gave no indication of whether the information was complimentary or uncomplimentary.

The legality of acting in this way was upheld by the Court of Appeal some years later when three judges headed by Lord Denning, Master of the Rolls, repealed a temporary injunction brought by two shipping companies after the Baltic Exchange had posted notices telling members that the secretary had information about them which could be of use to those contemplating doing business with them.

In March 1982 they ruled that the Exchange (and the International Maritime Bureau, formed in 1981, who had acted similarly) could issue warnings to its members about shipping companies even in the absence of concrete proof of the fraud. Even if they were not certain that a fraudster was involved with a shipping company, said Lord Denning, it was right that interested parties should learn of the Exchange's suspicions if there were 'reasonable grounds for an honest belief that he may be'. It was very necessary to have someone to fight fraud.

Most foreign firms of consequence in the world of shipping had offices in London, and were themselves overseas associates of the Exchange or, if not, were represented by full members. The ethical framework to the conduct of international business provided by the Baltic Exchange was therefore almost entirely a matter of self-discipline. The directors who applied the code were elected from among members. No other institution of a similar kind anywhere in the world had gone to the trouble of establishing this degree of regulation. That the ultimate penalty of expulsion from membership of the Baltic Exchange in 1974 was still so great a deterrent to unbecoming behaviour, and that it was still not considered necessary to define 'unbecoming', or to spell out what was meant by 'the character of a member', was a tribute to the tenacity of men like William Wilson, Benjamin Lancaster, Septimus Glover, Stephen Ralli, Bridges Webb and the rest; to an ideal which, setting higher standards than required by British law, transcended time and nationality. The existence at the Baltic of a deep-rooted and strictly enforced tradition of commercial probity and financial reliability, without parallel in any other city in the world, was a major contribution to the continuing strength of the London freight market.

What price a 'firm offer' in Tokyo, New York or Antwerp? In these places the ultimate deterrent was prosecution under the laws of the land. Anyone who made a verbal firm offer felt entitled to withdraw it if he wished before it expired and before he had confirmed it in writing, not that he would necessarily always do so. The law allowed him to, and there was no other sanction which constrained him to act otherwise. The Baltic member however, though legally entitled to, never did so unless he was set on committing commercial suicide.

The broker member acting for his shipowner client gave a firm offer of a ship to a merchant who had bought 30,000 tons of grain in America and found a buyer in Holland. The broker made his offer on the Floor of the Baltic at 11.45 a.m., say, for reply by 4 p.m. the same day. Legally he could withdraw it if, in the meantime, he received a better offer – a voyage from the River Plate, say, at a better return. But the merchant who had chartered the ship knew that the firm offer, coming from a member of the Baltic, would not be withdrawn, and that it was his until that evening without confirmation in writing. It would have been the same if the offer had come over the telephone and not been given face to face.

In house purchase nothing was 'final' until the contract was signed. Verbal offer and acceptance meant nothing. At the Baltic it meant everything. The knowledge that the transport 'prop' of his transaction was firm, and that he could rely on it entirely, enabled the broker to proceed at once, without waiting until the next evening, with the negotiations which made up the deal. He knew an offer without ifs and buts, and without puzzling provisos, was firm, although every other aspect of the transaction might be shifting. He knew he could hitch his sale on this unmovable peg. To do deals in a market where this was taken for granted halved the time required to do business elsewhere. On the Baltic a fixture was a fixture from the moment it was confirmed verbally, without the immediate need for a signed agreement.

Charterers and shipowners used the Baltic because of the reputation earned for its service which businessmen of goodwill had built up so conscientiously over the years – a reputation in danger of being allowed to evaporate through neglect, through lack of vigilance. Those who had a vested interest in making sure that never happened, such as Derek Prentis, knew that the volume of business they transacted derived from it: 'The nucleus of chartering was done by a few people in those days, and of course the question of ethical failure was unheard of. The feelings of members were the same as 100 years ago. They were proud to be members of the Exchange and would do nothing to harm its worldwide reputation.'

There was no written code of conduct, but the concern of the directors that no one should doubt such a code's existence, the value they placed on members adhering to it, and the means they had for making sure they did if they wished to retain their membership, were spelled out unequivocally in the rules which were redrafted in 1968 and 1971.

Women were admitted to membership in 1974, and in 1976 a major revision of the rules reduced the minimum age of admission to 19 by the introduction of probationers. At the same time, to the dismay of some of the older members, chartering clerks were renamed 'representatives'. Additionally, foreigners with a residential qualification of three years in the United Kingdom were allowed entry to the Exchange as representatives. A regrouping of trade associations connected with the Exchange led to the formation of the Federation of Oils, Seeds and Fats Association (FOSFA) and of the Grain and Feed Trade Association (GAFTA). Both of these had their offices in the Baltic Exchange building, as did the Institute of Chartered Shipbrokers.

In the 1970s it seemed for a time that the free trade, by which international shipping and shipbroking flourished, was in danger of contracting. There was a fear that the governments of the European Common Market (established without Britain by the Treaty of Rome, signed in 1957), alarmed at the prospect of Japan being able to supply between 80 and 90 per cent of the world's new tonnage by 1980, might rule that cargoes bound for Europe must be carried in European-built ships. Would the United States government, anxious to nurse its expanding shipbuilding industries, pass legislation of a similar nature?

When the High Level Group set up by the Organization for Economic Co-operation and Development (OECD) published its report in September 1972, the 'one world' conception of the open economic order of the wartime Atlantic Charter embodied in the Bretton Woods agreement of 1944, and the later General Agreement on Tariffs and Trade (GATT), seemed to be in jeopardy. Free trade was the post-war ideal towards which the rules of world commerce were to progress by staged negotiations. But, when in August 1971 President Nixon announced the suspension of the dollar's notional convertibility into gold and imposed a temporary 10 per cent import surcharge, it looked as if the spirit of economic nationalism was taking over after all.

However, the declaration of the nine heads of state or government of the enlarged European Community at their summit meeting in October 1972 was propitious. 'The Community reaffirms its determination to encourage the development of international trade', stated paragraph 5. The Community was ready to participate in the open-minded spirit it had already shown and, according to the procedures laid down by the International Monetary Fund (IMF) and GATT, in negotiations based on the principle of reciprocity. Paragraph 12 set out the steps the Community were determined to take with regard to the industrial countries 'to ensure the harmonious development of world trade'.

> To contribute, while respecting what has been achieved by the Community, to a progressive liberalisation of international trade by measures based on reciprocity and relating to both tariffs and non-tariff barriers. To maintain a constructive dialogue with the United States, Japan, Canada and its other industrialised trade partners in a forthcoming spirit, using the most appropriate methods.

For a long time, Britain had a huge deep-sea trade carrying grain across the North Atlantic to ports in the UK. But then Britain became a grain exporter to the tune of many millions of tons, mostly in short hauls to Europe – with which Britain's trade had become more preoccupied.

Tables and benches (right) at which brokers and traders could talk business face to face were reminders of the Baltic's coffee house origins.

And that had a significant effect on British involvement in the shipping business which, though the ownership of the tonnage is no longer the salient thing as far as the Baltic is concerned, still had relevance. As Derek Walker, secretary of the Baltic from 1968 to 1992, sees it, the trade and the ships go together: 'The influence of the nation over its own trade and tonnage is important. The Baltic's pre-eminence is to a degree related to the scale of the UK's involvement in shipowning and the UK's own involvement in world trade. However both are factors which have ceased to be as significant as they were.'

Derek Walker, secretary of the Baltic Exchange from 1968 to 1992.

When Peter Warwick joined the Baltic in the early 1950s there were some eighty British deep-sea tramp shipowners, and there were a number of brokers who made a living just by fixing British ships. Many of these owners were relatively small family businesses owning perhaps two or three ships, and there were few publicly quoted British tramp shipowners.

Fixing the ships and working the market was a much more leisurely affair then. A session on the Baltic ran from 11.45 a.m. until lunch-time, and there was a half-hour session from 4 p.m. until 4.30 p.m. Before going on the Floor in the morning members often had a cup of coffee in the coffee room.

Peter Warwick remembers being encouraged to join one of the regular coffee tables, since in that way – as well as walking the Floor – friendships were forged and contacts made which were to prove invaluable in the future. Once on the Floor he would almost certainly become involved in conducting actual negotiations: 'It was rare for anything to be exchanged in writing between the parties concerned until the charter was drawn up. Also, unlike today, ships were not normally run spot, although there were specialists in this field as now. But offers generally had to be made with a reply time measured in hours, if not the next day.'

It was even more leisurely when his great-grandfather J J C Warwick joined the Baltic at South Sea House as an employee of Jackson Brothers and Cory of West Hartlepool, to be followed in 1896 by his grandfather John Warwick, who worked for Bucknall Brothers, the shipowners who were taken over by Sir John Ellerman in 1908.

> My father's family came from Hartlepool on the North East coast which was where many tramp shipowners were based in the latter part of the 19th century. In 1886 there were some 50 deep-sea tramp shipowners established in Hartlepool mainly on the back of the coal trade. The export of coal from the UK was of tremendous importance to the tramp shipping industry in the late 19th and early 20th centuries, and I have always maintained that the growth and indeed the decline of the British trampship industry was based on two factors, the coal trade and the Empire.

Short hauls or long deep-sea ones, to Europe or to the Americas, the business of brokers on the Baltic was, and is, measured in terms of the value of the fixtures which they can make, irrespective of their nature. The invisible earnings yielded by their services mounted towards the end of the 1970s in a remarkable way. The £181 million which the Exchange earned in 1980 rose to £285 million the following year, a useful contribution to the City of London's £3,452 million, which had risen more than 50 per cent from the £2,275 million of the year before.

The maintenance of that level of earnings stemmed from the volume of business the Baltic attracted by virtue of being the centre of that business. New York and Tokyo tried to establish similar centres, as did Hamburg, Piraeus, Paris and Hong Kong. But a circle can only have one centre. To attempt to line up the world's freight demands against the supply available in more than one place at one time brought confusion and anarchy. It proved impractical. As soon as an enquiry, other than a local one, was received in the New York or Tokyo Exchange, their first reaction was to find out what was available in London. With communications as efficient as they were, the location of an Exchange that served the world was immaterial, but the Baltic was there first. Not

Key players on the home-grown grain ring (clockwise from left) – William Englebright, Alf Hooker, Alan Harper, Geoff Coley, and Harold Johnson.

Chairman Peter Tudball (overleaf) addresses members on the Floor following his election in June 1991.

only that; it had been there very much longer than any other similar Exchange. It had an accumulation of expertise shared by no other. The continuing need for the Baltic derived from its historical role as the point of reference for the world.

Its eminence was enhanced by being on the Greenwich Meridian. Since it is impossible for every country on the sphere to have night at the same time, wherever the Exchange was located there would always be half of the world at work while its own doors were closed for the night. But to be on the dividing line between East and West brought considerable advantages. In the morning business with the East could be concluded before lunch, leaving the afternoon free to deal with the Americans – the New York market opened at 2 p.m. British time.

Americans had no two minds about the 'unique importance' of the Baltic Exchange. It was there, said a writer in the journal of the American Bureau of Shipping, *Surveyor*, in May 1976:

> that more information is available and more face to face personal contact takes place than anywhere in the world. ... Its members are confident that the Baltic Exchange will remain a key factor in shaping international commerce, and agree with an observation in an article in *Barron's*, the weekly financial newspaper, that there is no effective substitute for the services it offers.

The Exchange was the focus of the international freight market.

The Exchange's position on the Greenwich Meridian was an advantage in both the dry and the wet market. For a broker to make a fixture in the latter, however, he needed very much less time. Those in tanker business traditionally did their fixing on the telephone or by Telex in the office. Negotiating terms in the dry cargo market could take a week.

In the tanker market a broker might start 'working' a ship at, say, 2.30 in the afternoon and have completed by 4.30 p.m. Tanker charter-parties are very precise, covering all the requirements of the trade. There are fewer charterers in the tanker market, so there is less need for an area where a lot of people discuss individual types of business. It is all very much more compact than dry cargo.

Smaller tankers act as tramp ships, picking up cargo wherever they can. But the main business is done by VLCCs of between 250,000 and 500,000 tonnes, carrying crude oil only, for which there are only twenty loading places in the whole world. They tend therefore to go backwards and forwards on a route, laden one way, ballast back.

The whole operation is helped by brokers in the tanker business being able to work on the published schedule of freight rates from load port to discharge port, known as 'Worldscale'. In the dry cargo market the owner works out the rate for each separate voyage in dollars and cents. For wet cargo, Worldscale computes an agreed flat rate, and negotiations on fixing the ship take the form of discussing what the rate will be as a percentage of that – 'Worldscale 50', half the published rate; 'Worldscale 200', twice the rate. There is no need for lengthy negotiation. It is all worked out in the published schedule, in the possession of both shipowners and ship charterers, calculated on the basis of a certain return per day.

Before World War 2 the rates for the bulk carrying of oil in ocean tankers under voyage charters were negotiated and agreed in terms of shillings and pence, or dollars, per ton. During the war the British government requisitioned all British flag vessels, including tankers, which they made available to the major oil companies from time to time. Freight for voyages performed by vessels under this arrangement was therefore payable to the British government, whose Ministry of Transport devised a series of freight rate schedules. This MoT schedule on a range-to-range basis remained in place, along with government control of shipping, after the war ended. In the USA, where the government had also requisitioned flag tankers, similar freight rate schedules were issued.

> The tanker trade had come to recognise the advantages of having schedules of freight rates so that rates could be freely negotiated without the waste of time and possibility of error involved in specifying many different rates in a charter that covered a number of voyages. With the ensuing free market a system evolved of quoting on the basis of the MoT or United States Maritime Commission (USMC) rates plus or minus a percentage as dictated by market conditions. Clearly such a system facilitated the swift negotiation of business. (*The Development of Tanker Rate Schedules*, The International Tanker Nominal Freight Scale Association and the Association of Ship Brokers and Agents, 1973)

At the instigation of Shell and BP, in November 1952 the London market tanker nominal freight scale was issued, and it remained in force until 1954. It became 'Intascale' from 1962 to 1969 and, from 1969, 'Worldscale', jointly sponsored and issued by the International Tanker Nominal Freight Scale Association in London and the Association of Ship Brokers and Agents (Worldscale) Inc. in New York.

The more protracted negotiations which brokers in the dry cargo market had to conduct earned them the same 1¼ per cent commission as the tanker brokers. And brokers who acted for merchants who chartered ships to carry grain, iron ore and phosphates at a future date had, in addition to the complications of agreeing a satisfactory fixture, the worry that the price quoted in advance, and accepted, would be greater than the one they would have to pay when the voyage took place a year later. That would turn the profit on the sale of the commodity in question into a loss. The broker of the shipowner involved in that deal would be worried that the advance price he had quoted for the chartering of his ship in a year's time, which he had to stick to, would be below that which he would have charged at the time of the voyage, bringing *him* a loss.

A merchant could protect himself against fluctuations in freight charges by buying a ship of his own in which to carry his merchandise. Without the capital to do that, by the end of 1985 he could buy 'freight futures' contracts which would in effect give some safeguard against rising freight rates in coming months. This was possible through the Baltic International Freight Futures Exchange (BIFFEX). The major differences between buying a ship and taking a position on the futures market were that futures were traded on margin, whereas ships need to be paid for in full and have a daily cost to keep them running, compared to a 'paper' freight contract that represents only a change in the value of the freight. The major attraction of freight futures contracts was that by subsequently taking the equal but opposite action, a bought contract could be resold, the only obligation remaining being that of receiving profits or paying losses, always in cash.

The machinery for trading on the market price for freight as much as two years ahead, whether for speculation or to 'lay off' risk, was devised by members of the London futures industry, with the involvement of the Baltic, at a very early stage. Following a lengthy investigation period which included highly complex analyses of ocean freight movements and trends, the market opened for business in dry cargo freight on the Floor of the Baltic Exchange in 1985.

The background to – and the most important part of – the operation of the market was the production of the Baltic Freight Index (BFI). Representative quotes for a list of pre-defined routes covering varying commodities from the dry cargo sector would be gathered from a panel made up of experts chosen from the major shipbroking members of the Exchange. Every day they prepared and submitted their indications for the routes selected, numbering fifteen at the start, and by applying well-publicised fixed weighting factors, a single quotation was published representing the 'average' of the basket of routes and ship sizes making up the index.

The work involved for the panelists was demanding, of both time and effort. As Paul Douglas Powell, senior partner of Moore Stephens, explained in *The Baltic*, 'in the process of providing this daily report, the brokers themselves have to question and monitor their reasons for the rate for each route, since no broker would want to risk his reputation by giving an obviously erroneous rate'. The introduction of the futures contract was welcomed as a counter to the vagaries of unforeseen freight movements in the dry cargo market, and was expected to save both shipowners and charterers a considerable amount of money.

The co-ordinator for this gathering of information, the Baltic freight

The freight futures market at the London Commodity Exchange in the 1990s.

reporter, was Michael Phillips up to 1993, and it was he who made sure the reports were received on time, checked them for obvious errors and omissions, and then fed them into the computer for the mathematical formulae to be applied, and thus produced the index for that day.

> The Index is traded on BIFFEX for specified future settlement months by open negotiation between willing buyers and sellers on the 'floor' of the market. The price being quoted for each contract month will constantly change in line with supply and demand from the market, hence the prices will reflect the views of investors in the market as to what the settlement price for the futures contract position will be and, thereby, what the level of the physical market will be at that time. (BIFFEX Information Card, January 1992)

In 1986, BIFFEX opened a contract for trading tanker futures, but there was no perceived need to 'hedge' the risk on oil cargoes, and that contract was subsequently suspended.

The business of other members of the Baltic was international dealing in commodities, very often as members of the various trade associations which maintained offices in the Baltic building. These associations included the Grain and Feed Trade Association (GAFTA), formed by the amalgamation of the London Corn Trade and the Animal Feeding Stuffs Associations, as well as the Federation of Oils, Seeds and Fats Association (FOSFA).

Futures markets were no strangers to the commodity section of the Baltic, there having been a coarse grain futures market of one description or another on the Floor of the Exchange since 1929. To quote from *The London Grain Futures Market*, a study by Graham L Rees, D W Colenutt and C J Redston, which was published in March 1976, 'unlike Topsy, who "just growed", futures markets emerged to meet a need'.

It can be said that futures markets in a form still recognisable today have been in existence since the mid-1850s when the Chicago Board of Trade commenced trading. In the UK, the first grain market started for wheat in 1883 in Liverpool, and to some considerable extent this produced the need for a 'central clearing system' to ensure good deliveries of produce based on a system of deposits. This first guaranteeing body, which was the forerunner of the futures clearing operations in London, was brought about by a group of financiers, many of whom held names famous in the City and elsewhere. These honourable financiers included Arbuthnot Latham, Baring Brothers, William Brandt & Sons, Hambros, Kleinworts, Huths, Rothschilds and Henry Schroder.

The guarantee system set up was known as the London Produce Clearing House Ltd and 'the object of the company was to place on a secure basis, by a system of deposits, the dealing in produce for future delivery, which has become such an important development both in Europe and America'.

The paths of the Baltic and the futures industry were first destined to cross in 1929 when the first futures contract started trading, on the Floor of the Exchange, for Manitoba wheat. After an interruption caused by war, trading on the futures market on the Baltic was resumed in January 1954, covering coarse grain contracts for wheat and barley.

At this time it was still imported grain that formed the backbone of the

trade, with barley soon outgrowing maize – having traded, for example, 529,500 tons and 179,250 tons respectively. Those were the days when an observer would hear bids and offers in shillings and pence per quarter, instead of pounds per metric tonne. As a result of a growing UK grain crop, the market was changed to home-grown grain, both wheat and barley, in the mid-1960s.

Constructed in one corner of the Floor, the freight futures market eventually left the Baltic in 1991.

Stalwarts of the 'ring' on the Baltic at that time were Alfred A Hooker and Geoffrey H Coley, later joined by Geoffrey Hunniset, and these were responsible for a tremendous amount of futures trade which continued through the change of the market from home-grown grain to EEC grain in the 1972/3 season. This coincided with a complete overhaul of the market rules, again spearheaded by the efforts of Alf Hooker. Shortly after, in 1974, Geoff Coley ceased trading as a sole trader and formed a new futures broking company with Alan Harper, which was to continue until the company was sold in 1987. The company of A A Hooker & Co. Ltd was also sold in the mid-1980s, with both of these sales indicating further changes to come.

As a result of a change in climate in the investment industry, which brought about the Financial Services Act in 1988, costs appeared to increase considerably while turnover went down, causing some stress in all of the Baltic futures markets. In a previous period of concerted growth for the futures industry, additional futures markets were established at the

Baltic for main crop potatoes (1980), pig meat (1984), live cattle and early potatoes (1986), and for soya meal (1975) – although this market did not move to the Baltic until 1987. These were in addition to freight futures, already mentioned. The period 1973 until 1985 saw great activity for the rear of the Baltic trading Floor, where the markets were sited. Probably the busiest years witnessed were 1972/3 for wheat and barley, as a result of the 'Great Russian Grain Steal' when record volumes (often around 150,000 to 170,000 tonnes per day) were traded, and 1976/7 for potatoes as a result of the drought of 1976, when daily volumes often reached 75,000 tonnes.

Unfortunately, as a direct result of the Financial Services Act, all of the 'Baltic' markets were obliged to unite under the banner of the Baltic Futures Association, and all removed from the Baltic to be resited at Commodity Quay near the World Trade Centre, which is the home of the London Commodity Exchange. In recent times, trading volumes have been depressed.

The quality of the service which Baltic traders and shipbrokers were able to give their principals depended on receiving up-to-date information, and most of them made sure that their offices kept pace with all that was new in telecommunications technology. From 1989 they were able to benefit too from the decision of the Copenhagen-based Baltic and International Maritime Council (BIMCO) to locate at the Exchange the London end of the global maritime communications network conceived by the council's president, George Livanos. This was operated by a separate company, BIMCOM, of which BIMCO was a small shareholder, with the object of providing the world's shipping industry with quality information speedily. Livanos, and the BIMCOM management team he appointed, allied themselves with the Cable and Wireless subsidiary Mercury Communications and with INFONET, owned by eleven national post telegraph and telephone (PTT) companies, which gave their specialist circuit instant access to an existing system without having to find money to build their own. The Baltic Exchange rented them space on the third floor and in the basement at St Mary Axe from whence they began to transmit messages to all parts of the world.

Her Majesty The Queen sees the new grain ring in action.

It was not long before some two hundred shipping companies world-wide were making use of the BIMCOM International Maritime Communications Network, as well as leading brokerage houses. Among the first of the latter to avail themselves of the service were H Clarkson & Company and Angus Graham & Partners. A medium increasingly in demand was electronic mail and, for shipping documentation, electronic data interchange (EDI). BIMCOM have enabled their customers to enjoy considerable savings in their costs by having

Telex messages routed through the INMARSAT radio-by-satellite voice channel. BIMCOM is not, however, encouraging the development of a closed user group of shipping companies.

The aim of the shipowners engaged principally in the Baltic and White Sea trade who formed BIMCO in 1905 was the general 'furtherance of the well-being of the shipping industry'. It monitors the activities of the United Nations Conference on Trade & Development (UNCTAD) and the United Nations International Maritime Organization (IMO). It works with bodies such as the Customs Cooperation Council in formulating uniform rules to combat illegal drug trafficking. Like the Baltic, it strives to ensure that the documentation of international shipping is clearly drafted and balanced, and reflects the changing market place. It notifies its members of unfair charges. It collaborates, when the occasion requires, with the Federation of National Associations of Shipbrokers & Agents (FONASBA), formed in 1969 and also based in London, which has consultative status with UNCTAD at whose meetings in Geneva it speaks as the voice of shipbrokers and agents internationally. Like the British Chamber of Shipping, BIMCO has established a documentary committee to maintain the momentum which the shipping industry started in 1980 when it developed thirty-two definitions covering 'laytime' and other aspects of charter-party law.

Sir Ian Denholm, president of BIMCO, attended the Shipping Documentation Conference organised by the Baltic at St Mary Axe in December 1991 at which delegates were exhorted to take action before others, such as UNCTAD, acted for them. They then got down to discussing the need for them to revise outdated charter-parties such as the River Plate 'Centrocon', written in 1914; the 'Amwelsh', dating originally from seventy-five years before and not amended since 1979; the Gencon, the charter-party most used in the short sea trades, and specialised charter-parties used with bodies such as the World Food Organization of the United Nations.

By 1976 there was no longer enough unlet space at St Mary Axe to meet members' demands for offices. For five years the Exchange had been considering the possibility of selling its St Mary Axe freehold, which would have brought it around £14 million net, and providing members with a new, purpose-built complex containing an exchange, offices and ancillary accommodation. Indeed in 1972 they applied for, and received, an Office Development Permit.

The favourite idea was to purchase for £10 million a four-acre site adjacent to Cutler Street north of Houndsditch called Cutlers Gardens. On it were warehouses once owned by the Port of London Authority, listed buildings like St Mary Axe but now standing empty. It was reckoned that demolishing them and building a new complex, complete with the latest communications equipment and accounting for inflation, would cost in the region of £44 million. Completion was envisaged for 1980. There would be some 450,000 square feet of floor space. Since they estimated that development costs would have become more than £75 million by 1980, far beyond the Exchange's resources, they hoped they could sell the complex to financing institutions from whom they would lease it back, and be able to offer all the members already accommodated, plus those whose demands they could not meet, up-to-date office space at favourable rents.

In 1976 projected commercial rents to sustain the development were seen as being between £12 and £16 a square foot. Directors of the Baltic explored the project in detail, but few members were prepared to consider renting offices even at £10 to £12 a square foot. So chairman Basil Fehr announced from the rostrum at New Year in 1976 that the project was shelved.

The eventual purchaser of Cutler Street, English & Continental, went bankrupt within two years. Subsequently Greycoat Estates developed the site for the Standard Life Assurance Company. In 1979 further discussions took place about the Exchange occupying part of the redevelopment under the terms of the original Office Development Permit. By the end of that year the issue was closed, and the St Mary Axe site, listed in 1972 as of architectural or historic interest, was subsequently upgraded to Grade II★ (in 1987). This category of classification applied to particularly important buildings of more than special interest and was given to only around 4 per cent of listed buildings. From then on sale or development of the 1903 Baltic Exchange was more constrained.

Action of some kind was required, however, not only in members' interests but to increase the Exchange's income, and in 1977 the directors obtained planning consent to add another storey. Should they use it? A whole new floor of offices would certainly add to their rent income very substantially. Already it was providing more than half the Exchange company's total income – £831,000 in 1976/7 compared with £282,000 from members' subscriptions. By 1980 the income from property had risen to £1,183,000 out of a total of £2,171,000. With membership down from the 2,834 of 1977 to 2,388, the Baltic recorded a loss of £22,000 before taxation. They were reassured by the knowledge that their property had been valued at more than £10 million.

They made no reduction, however, in their charitable giving. In October 1979 they established by a trust deed the Baltic Charitable Fund for the purpose of supporting registered charities, particularly those connected with the business of the members of the Exchange and the City of London. Its capital was subscribed by the Baltic Exchange Ltd who donated income derived from government chartering. In 1994 the fund had assets of £1 million and every year it distributes some £55,000 to charities of its choice.

Other charities associated with the Baltic are the Baltic Exchange Charitable Society, established by trust deed in November 1978 with a view to combining the work of the Baltic Exchange Benevolent Society (formerly known as the Baltic Mercantile and Shipping Exchange and Shipping Benevolent Society) and the Cereals and Baltic Society (formerly known as the Cereals and Baltic Friendly Society). The members of both societies became members of the new society. On 28 February 1979 the Cereals and Baltic Society was formally wound up and all its assets and liabilities were transferred to the new society, and on 30 April 1984 the Baltic Exchange Benevolent Society was similarly wound up. The Cereals and Baltic Friendly Society was formed in 1909 and can trace its origins to the Cereals Dinner on 13 October 1885. The Baltic Exchange Benevolent Society was founded in 1912. The society's funds are derived from subscriptions, donations, legacies and interest and dividends on investments.

Membership of the society is restricted to members of the Baltic

Exchange and employees of member companies and staff of the Exchange itself, by payment of a life subscription of £30 or an annual subscription of £3. The object is to assist beneficiaries who must be members of the society, their spouses, widows, widowers, issue or other dependants who are in necessitous circumstances. The society has assets of £3.2 million and approximately two thousand members, and currently supports forty-two beneficiaries. The chairman and chief executive are *ex-officio* members of the committee which administers it.

The Corn Exchange Benevolent Society was established in 1863, to relieve need, hardship or distress for those who are or were engaged in the corn, grain, seed, cereal, animal feeding stuffs, pulses, malt, flour or granary-keeping trades together with their dependants at the time of their death. Funds are derived from subscriptions, donations, legacies and interest and dividends on its investments. Membership is restricted to those in the various trades connected with the Corn Exchange, by payment of a life subscription of £50 or an annual subscription of £5. The society has assets of £1.1 million and currently supports eighteen beneficiaries.

Baltic Exchange II, the Salcombe lifeboat supported by the Exchange. By 1994 the Exchange had helped the RLNI by sponsoring six lifeboats.

Founded in 1852, the London Shipowners and Shipbrokers' Benevolent Society, formerly known as the Shipbrokers' Benevolent Fund, grants relief for shipbrokers or shipowners and their dependants. The society's funds are derived from donations from shipbroking and shipowning companies and investment income, and there are assets of £400,000 and twelve beneficiaries.

Membership of the Oilseed, Oil and Feedingstuffs Trades Benevolent Association, formed in 1971, is open to permanent employees engaged in the oilseed, oil and feedingstuffs trades in the United Kingdom. Life membership is £50; or there is an annual subscription of £5.

In addition there are two very small charitable funds: the Bonno Krull Fund created by one of the original partners of H Clarkson & Company, a Norwegian, in June 1940; and the Shipbrokers Emergency Fund formed for the most part out of income earned from government chartering in the Great War, in 1918. All the charities associated with the Baltic are now administered by the secretary, Douglas Painter, from the Charities Office at the Exchange.

A charitable initiative that benefits all who travel by sea is the Exchange's support for the Royal National Lifeboat Institution. This began to take effect in 1888 when the first lifeboat sponsored by members, *Baltic*, began seven years' service at Wells in Norfolk. That boat was followed by two more, which were in operation until 1936. In 1970 another sponsored boat, *Baltic Exchange*, went into service at Salcombe; it saved more than sixty lives and over fifty craft over the years. Members contributed £35,000 towards it. A second Salcombe-based lifeboat, *Baltic Exchange II*, was named in 1989; over £100,000 was pledged by members towards its construction. In addition to that sum, through the annual lifeboat appeal members raise over £20,000 a year towards the running of the boat. In 1994 a donation of £100,000 was made by the Baltic Charitable Fund to mark the centenary of the City branch of the RNLI. The money, which came from commissions earned during the 1990–1 Gulf campaign for the liberation of Kuwait, will go towards a new boat to be stationed at Dover.

HM The Queen, with Peter Harding – chairman of the Baltic – is led on to the Floor in 1981 by the super-intendent, Leslie Goillau.

It was a mark of the Baltic's importance in the affairs of the nation when, on 9 December 1981, HM The Queen visited the Exchange, toured the Floor, and met members there and in the coffee room before lunching with Peter Harding, the chairman, and directors in the Queen's Room. The occasion marked the twenty-fifth anniversary of the opening by Her Majesty of the Queen's Room building in November 1956. Three years later HRH The Duke of Edinburgh made a similar tour of the Floor.

In April 1982 the institution changed its name from the Baltic Mercantile & Shipping Exchange Ltd, which it had been given when it was formed in 1903, to the Baltic Exchange Ltd, and also reregistered as a private company. It had not been to any extent a market place where merchants traded commodities (except in futures) since the 1970s. As a mainly ship chartering centre its income was hit by the continuing recession in world trade, and 1983 saw a reduction in membership to 2,248. The reputation of the Exchange still derived, however, from the quality and not the quantity of its membership. This was underlined that year when the directors ruled that in future all young probationers intending to work on the dry cargo freight market should be issued with a copy of the printed *Baltic Code*, and be examined on it before making the transition to representative status. Those under the age of 35 formed a young members' group in 1986. There were around 250 of that age at the time. Their aim was to inform themselves about the business, social and sporting events available to the London shipping community. The directors saw it as a forum for encouraging the future leaders to acknowledge the importance of the Exchange. Renamed the Young Baltic Association in 1992, it appointed a steering group under Betina Wettergren of H Clarkson & Company, who had been one of the prime movers of the group, to explore ways of developing it as an integral part of the Baltic Exchange.

Though total membership fell again in 1987, the income from property rose and was expected to improve even further. However, the directors thought better of using the planning consent they had gained to build another storey, and decided to exploit their assets in other ways. Radio telephones had already supplanted those pocket paging units, and now equipment was installed for facsimile transmission (fax) and plans made for data transmission. Members of the London Corn Exchange, who had been conducting their business since 1953 in the building on the site in Mark Lane where they had begun in 1750, moved to the Baltic Exchange in 1987. The arrangement was that, in return for a once-only capital payment, the company would provide the Corn Exchange with a market floor indefinitely. Corn Exchange members came to market only on Mondays between 11 a.m. and 3 p.m., with samples displayed on some fifty stands. In April the following year the 200-year-old operation was formally reopened on what had been the grain futures market area by the Lord Mayor of London. All members of the Corn Exchange became

The Baltic Exchange plays its part in the Lord Mayor's show of 1985, when the theme was 'service with a smile'.

Market day on the Corn Exchange at the Baltic in the late 1980s.

Jim Buckley, chief executive of the Baltic since 1992.

Betina Wettergren, a prime mover of the Young Baltic Association.

members of the Baltic. Seven years later they represented 8 per cent of the total membership.

Redevelopment was again considered in 1988, not by way of merely adding another floor but in a more ambitious way. Two years later, however, the directors thought it inappropriate to act on the new planning permission they had been given, and chose instead to 'refurbish' the building, particularly the façades. The Bury Street entrance and the St Mary Axe front were cleaned; the Floor was upgraded; new arbitration rooms were built and, in the basement, a City gym was installed.

In May 1991 Jim Buckley was appointed deputy secretary, part of his remit being to develop a new strategy. He had joined the scientific civil service in 1965 and, after serving as private secretary to three cabinet ministers, left it as an assistant secretary in 1985 to become chief executive of the British Veterinary Association. From 1987 until 1991 he was deputy director-general of the (British) Chamber of Shipping. The decision to have him succeed Derek Walker, with the title of chief executive, was taken in December 1991. Before that, Jim Buckley made the first move towards the Baltic's new strategy.

More importantly, he sought help from consultants to rethink the whole *raison d'être* of the Exchange. After the peak of 2,834 in 1977, membership was down below the two thousand mark in 1989 at 1,966, and in 1990 it fell again to 1,916. In that year, however, the turnover was £4,587,000, and they paid a dividend of £1.10, 10 pence more than in the previous year. In 1992 the Exchange had only 1,749 members.

The strategic business review, commissioned from business consultants PRAGMA under the Department of Trade and Industry enterprise initiative scheme submitted in March 1992, warned that, with the property market continuing to be depressed, the Exchange would lose tenants as well and would suffer a 'worst-case' pre-tax loss of £1.3 million by 1993/4. The offices, for which top City rent was being charged, were old and of poor quality, and their rental income was vital to the Exchange. Sixty tenants in the main building, 14–20 St Mary Axe, and 19–21 Bury Street, produced an income of almost £3 million, most on long leases at rents of £25 to £35 per square foot.

The Baltic Exchange needed to reposition itself, said PRAGMA, in a role not focused so specifically around members' trading activities: 'To a large extent the requirement for regular daily or weekly inter-personal contact to facilitate trading has gone.' The future of the Exchange lay in building on its reputation for adherence to high ethical standards, and on self-regulation and its code of conduct. They saw the Exchange moving the focus away from direct trading and more to becoming a leading international commercial members' club. They pointed out: 'As computer systems become more sophisticated, the Trading Floor will become less and less relevant.' They suggested the object now should be to unlock the income-generating potential of freehold building assets worth at least £35 million, and make the Baltic 'the pre-eminent business club in the City of London', with world-wide membership. Development of the building for that purpose would cost in the region of £55 million. The Exchange could continue profitably as it was for another ten years, but then it would gradually lose its appeal and the custom of the remaining members – the current rationale of the institution – would fade away.

They pointed to the danger surrounding the reluctance of members to accept the need for change until it was too late, of postponing the inevitable need to reconsider the whole purpose and function of the Baltic's trading activities.

At their board meeting on the morning of Friday 10 April, the chairman Peter Tudball and the directors discussed the implications of PRAGMA's report with their property advisers. They considered bringing in a developer to develop the site on the lines suggested by PRAGMA, but did not feel it would be viable. Whatever way they tackled the problem of transforming the site into a new complex, it would be a very expensive exercise and the result would probably not be satisfactory. Would it not perhaps be more sensible, they thought, to conserve the 1903 building with its trading Floor, which was only two storeys high, and also the façade, and redevelop the rest? The directors agreed to adopt the main thrusts of PRAGMA's strategy. 'The Board now has fire in its belly', remarked one of the Greek directors. 'We are not going to let this opportunity slip as we have in the past.' They moved into the dining room and sat down thirteen to lunch.

The Floor was being hired more and more by outside bodies for social occasions and business conferences, and there had been a booking that night for a gathering of three hundred ophthalmic surgeons, but they had changed the date to the day before.

Which was lucky.

At 9.20 p.m. a bomb consisting of 100 pounds of Semtex wrapped in a ton of fertiliser exploded in a van parked outside the 28 St Mary Axe entrance, having been placed there, as part of their terrorist campaign for a united Ireland, by members of the Irish Republican Army (IRA). It was the largest bomb ever planted and detonated on the British mainland. The blast blew the façade of the Baltic Exchange forward without demolishing it, and caused the front of the adjacent Chamber of Shipping building to collapse into the street. It killed 49-year-old Tom Casey, one of the senior attendants; and severely injured Ron Brooks, the caretaker, and also Jeffrey Blum of Prochart Services, a member, who was leaving the building at the moment of the explosion. It destroyed the offices of major companies in the Exchange building and rendered unoccupiable the Floor, the lower ground floor catering and banqueting areas and the offices of the secretariat. It also wrecked the whole of the sophisticated communications system. Chairman, directors, secretary, staff and members heard of the event on the ten o'clock Independent Television News. It put all plans for the future of the Baltic on indefinite hold.

Sir Maersk McKinney-Møller CBE enters the Floor with chairman Peter Tudball to the applause of members before receiving his honorary membership in 1991.

FIVE

TIGHT, STAUNCH AND STRONG

for all the havoc at St Mary Axe

The granite entrance of 28 St Mary Axe surrounded by debris from the upper floors stands gaunt against the crumpled face of the Chamber of Shipping building.

I t was the weekend. The chairman and deputy secretary were round at St Mary Axe at ten o'clock the next morning to survey the scene of devastation, along with the director-general of the Chamber of Shipping. They were soon joined by the vice-chairman and members of the staff. It was not until six o'clock that evening that a fireman found the body of Tom Casey in the front cloakroom from which television viewers had seen the injured Ron Brooks being carried the night before. On Sunday the chairman took up the offer of the chairman of Lloyd's to put an office at the disposal of the secretariat from which they could receive the many enquiries which poured in from all around the globe after news of the bomb outrage spread. By 10.30 a.m. on Sunday the Baltic Exchange had been restored to communication with the outside world. Key records were rescued from the debris and taken to Lime Street. Staffs of the sixty companies who leased offices in the main building and in Baltic Exchange Chambers recovered computers and discs, a large number of which – they were surprised to find – were still in working order. With so many empty offices in and around the City, they had little difficulty in finding willing landlords to give them office space – for the most part, rent free. The Chamber of Shipping were accommodated by the Vestey Group.

The Lord Mayor of London volunteered whatever assistance was needed, and Monday found the secretary of the Baltic Exchange, the deputy secretary and staff installed in Lloyd's of London, on a floor across the gallery on level 4 at Lime Street, equipped – through the efficiency of the Corporation of Lloyd's staff – with telephones, faxes, Telex equipment, lighting and heating, and with access to the building's catering. On Wednesday a trading floor opened alongside the secretariat, where that afternoon some seven hundred members, many flying in from overseas, assembled to hear a report from their board of directors, who had met in the morning with their architect and insurers. They were told that the Exchange would not have to be demolished, and that the offices at 14–20 St Mary Axe and 19–21 Bury Street, and at the back of the Exchange, were all structurally undamaged and capable of being restored. Tenants were under an obligation to reoccupy reinstated offices within the period of their lease if the Baltic acted with due despatch in repairing them. But rent ceased from 10 April, the day when the offices were not capable of being occupied. The buildings and contents were covered by insurance, as well as loss of gross rental income, plus £2 million over two years for the extra cost of working during disruption. The chairman said that of the possible alternative homes the Royal Exchange, the Corn Exchange and Lloyd's seemed unlikely. More suitable, he thought, would be the restored fish market at Billingsgate on the Thames, which members were invited to visit.

It was clear that rebuilding the 90-year-old Exchange would take many years. The granite and Portland stone façade was badly damaged and dislodged from the front building, which included the entrance lobby and four floors of offices. The Floor was structurally sound but much marble had been dislodged; all the domes were shattered. The five stained-glass windows of the memorial dome were completely destroyed, with a third of the hall dome blown away. Doors, partitions, ceilings and services of the offices were ruined. Almost every window was blown out, and the frames were buckled or torn. As a result of the IRA's act of terror, from 10 April there were no longer jobs for staff employed at St Mary Axe in catering, telecommunications, security, cleaning and administration. The board made generous financial arrangements for the ninety-two staff whom they had to make redundant.

On the temporary Floor at Lloyd's of London, Tom Mennear, the deputy superintendent, notes down a call from a member's office.

It was a sombre meeting, enlightened however by the telegram which the chairman read out from John Hadjipateras, chairman of the Greek Shipping Co-operation Committee.

> We share with you, together with the whole membership and friends of the Baltic both here and overseas, your great sorrow, caused by the despicable action which resulted in the extensive damage to the great shipping monument I once described as the high temple of the international shipping industry. With your inspiration and guidance, and the help of all devotees of the Baltic tradition, I am sure we shall soon see the Baltic in its original splendour.

In a joint letter to *Lloyd's List*, *The Times*, *The Daily Telegraph* and other national newspapers, Peter Tudball, chairman of the Baltic, and Michael Everard, president of the Chamber of Shipping, expressed their gratitude for the great efforts made by all the emergency services to recover casualties, secure dangerous buildings, clear away hazardous debris and

Damage to the upper floors of the Exchange, occupied by member companies, was extensive. Furniture and fittings were reduced to rubble at the front.

police the area, and to British Telecom for maintaining essential communications. They thanked too Guy's and St Bartholomew's Hospitals for responding so effectively in receiving and treating the injured. They expressed their gratitude for the leadership of the Lord Mayor, and for the swift response of David Coleridge, the chairman of Lloyd's, and Edmund Vestey, the chairman of the Vestey Group, who had quickly housed their two organisations.

Their two institutions, they were able to write on Easter Day, 21 April, were functional again.

> Our buildings will be restored or replaced. The Grade II listed trading floor of the Baltic Exchange shows no structural damage and will be sympathetically restored. We believe that the immense goodwill and unstinting kindness of everyone to all who have suffered from this act of great evil will reinforce the City's spirit of unity and strengthen its links, not least those between our two organisations.

After many months of negotiation with the insurers, assisted by Cyril Sweett & Partners, the Baltic directors decided to seek a lump sum indemnity settlement rather than a reinstatement of the complex of buildings as they had been before the explosion. The offices were for the most part sub-standard and, as the chairman said in his statement for the ninety-second annual general meeting of the Exchange in June 1993, 'the site must in due course be ripe for redevelopment'.

Emergency scaffolding is erected to hold up the collapsing façade, which can be seen separating from the building.

Even the Baltic's Rolls-Royce, parked underground, did not escape.

In November 1992 the directors agreed to accept a cash payment of £27.6 million, comprising £22.8 million for the buildings and contents, and £4.8 million for loss of incoming rent and business disruption.

> The Board is looking at many options for the reinstatement of different areas of the Exchange buildings. Given the many uncertainties which include the Exchange's future business requirements, constraints imposed by English Heritage and the state of the property market in the City, it is not yet possible to determine the exact reinstatement programme. (Chairman's statement, dated 26 May 1993)

The traditional income and expenditure structure of the Exchange disappeared on 10 April 1992. Income from property ceased overnight, as

Fragments from the plasterwork of the ceiling of the main Floor.

Property manager Brian Lawton pieces together fragments of marble in the elaborate jigsaw of reconstruction.

did income from catering. But the costs of staffing remained fixed until redundancies took effect at the end of June 1992. The cash received from the insurance settlement generated more than £400,000 in interest between December 1992 and May 1993, and was expected to earn around £1 million in interest over the following twelve months. Together with the remaining loss-of-rent insurance, the company saw this as bringing them a substantial profit for 1993/4. However, as the cash was spent on reinstating the Exchange, the interest they received would reduce significantly. The loss of rental income would have been exhausted by 1995. To ensure a secure future the profits of the next two years would have to be retained within the company. In the short term money was being consumed on living expenses and the immediate job of making the buildings safe. Extra expenditure on accommodation at Lloyd's amounted to more than £1 million, while building took a further £2 million by April 1993. Refurbishing part of 14–20 St Mary Axe for occupation by that month cost some £750,000. There were, however, some compensating savings in so far as the Exchange was not being used.

The shape of that future had long been a matter of discussion among members and directors. The IRA's action in no way forced the Baltic to change direction, nor did their detonating an even larger bomb a year later in Bishopsgate near the NatWest tower, causing the Baltic another

Derek Walker, Jack's son, proudly receives from Peter Tudball the illuminated vellum signifying his honorary membership in June 1992.

Jack Walker, 1902–91, secretary of the Exchange 1954–68.

£50,000-worth of damage and slight injury to two security staff. A joint fund known as Pool Re, amounting to some £200 million, had been created by the Department of Trade, Lloyd's and major insurance companies to meet the costs of rebuilding in the wake of renewed attack.

No one ever expected the debate on the Baltic's future to be short; it had from the start involved the 'development' of the St Mary Axe site, and the fact that the explosion had accelerated the process still left unanswered the question of how, though it certainly concentrated the mind. 'Everyone involved in the Baltic', wrote the chairman in the first issue of the institution's magazine, 'wants to retain the identity of the Exchange, and the criteria ultimately must be to find a place which will enable both members and staff to operate until a decision is made on the move back to our listed Exchange.' He continued:

> I have been heartened by the response of all the members who wish to keep the unity and identity of the market. This is the prime aim of the Baltic Board. I have also seen many members, who were not regular attenders at St Mary Axe, on the new Floor at Lloyd's and they have all expressed the wish that the Exchange continues to provide its usual outstanding service to the shipping industry. I will keep the membership fully informed of all developments, and what I can promise them is that the Floor will be restored to its original condition. There is no doubt that we will survive and thrive.

In the meantime the international freight market with its associated facilities continued without break in time, only in location, on the fourth-floor gallery in Lloyd's Lime Street building, where some four hundred to five hundred members attended on Mondays and Tuesdays. It was business as usual except for a change in the key position of secretary and chief executive. Derek Walker retired in June 1992 after serving the Exchange for thirty-six loyal years, twenty-four as secretary, having succeeded his father Jack Walker in the post in 1968. Presenting him with an illuminated vellum recording his admission to the ranks of honorary members, Peter Tudball paid tribute to his integrity, honesty and service. Douglas Painter, who had also served thirty-six years with the Exchange, became secretary to the charitable societies, and Miss A V M Gregory was appointed company secretary in the following year.

Although he had completed his normal two-year period of service, Peter Tudball, who was awarded the CBE, was elected to serve a third term as chairman until June 1994. To help him, his new chief executive and fellow directors to focus on the role which the Baltic should play in circumstances which had been changing at a pace few would have forecast in the 1960s, the board commissioned the PRAGMA consultancy to carry out a second survey, this time on likely membership needs, and to make further recommendations on general strategy.

PRAGMA sent 1,700 questionnaires to members and convened five discussion groups in June and July 1992. Just under five hundred were completed and returned – representing 30 per cent of the membership. Some felt that the international standing of the Exchange was no longer as strong as it had been; others felt standards had deteriorated, and that the board were not tough enough in dealing with offenders, that sanctions were 'a toothless threat' and 'a lion without claws'. One member declared: 'It is

A crowded Monday on the Floor in 1994. The Exchange reoccupied the Queen's Room on 5 April 1993 as a Floor for members.

still relying on the erroneous belief that it is the centre of world shipping. It has failed to act decisively and with vigour as world shipping policeman.'

From their answers to the questionnaire, it appeared that those who returned it felt the role of the Exchange was that of a business venue – the old term had been 'commercial resort' – and information exchange rather than a social club. There was no longer a need for a variety of catering options; social and club-type facilities – a gym, a swimming pool, overnight accommodation – were not needed by a large proportion of those who answered. Most of them did not want to return to the Baltic Exchange of the past, but to one revitalised with a stronger business and shipping focus. Three-quarters of them chose, out of the six options suggested, to go back to St Mary Axe by early 1993 with the Queen's Room as trading Floor and with basic bar and catering facilities only.

In the medium to long term, they said they would like to see the Exchange developing added-value services such as database systems and library and information services with a librarian and researchers; and publishing newsletters, research reports and a specialist journal. They would like to see insurance and indemnity services developed, and inter-member financial settlements. They advocated training, the mounting of a world-wide seminar and conference organisation. The Baltic, they said, should seek affiliations with, and provide services for, other international shipping and trade bodies.

PRAGMA's recommendation was that the Baltic should seek specialist partners with whom to develop such services rather than develop them itself. Such specialists – for example, a telecommunications company, a software house, and a training specialist – would benefit from the association with the Exchange through its world-wide status and image.

The consultancy's conclusion was:

> The *raison d'être* of the Baltic Exchange has always been to facilitate the business dealings of its members. In the past this could most advantageously be done through the provision of an open market. In the new technologically based trading environment of today, the Baltic's role remains the same – only the means of execution differs. Members have clearly stated that they still want Information, Communication and the sense of being part of a professional body. They value immensely the opportunity to make personal contacts and exchange informal market information in appropriate surroundings. The Baltic Exchange is still the only organisation and venue which can provide this for the vast majority of the membership.

The wish of members to return to St Mary Axe as swiftly as possible was acted upon with due punctiliousness. The board appointed Walter Lilly & Company of Thornton Heath main contractor for the dismantling of the Exchange building, working to the directions of Green Lloyd & Partners as architects and Ove Arup as structural engineers, under the supervision of project managers Cyril Sweett. They finished on 1 March 1993, three weeks ahead of programme.

In January 1993 they found the objects which the directors of the Exchange had chosen to place in the foundation stone when it was laid

on 25 June 1901 by the Lord Mayor of London, Frank Green, with the words 'May the structure to be raised upon it be creditable alike to the architects and builders, and may it fulfil also the purpose which you all deeply desire it to fill.' Queen Victoria had died three days before. Although President Kruger had fled to Europe and the Transvaal had been formally annexed by Britain, Boer guerrilla raids on British outposts continued with growing intensity, events that coloured the news columns of *The Times* and other newspapers of 25 June 1901 which were rescued from inside the stone where they had been placed as part of a 'time capsule'. With them were the business cards of the clerk of

Newspapers, coins, a grain sample jar and visiting cards recovered from the 1901 'time capsule'.

the works, general foreman and surveyor, and, as someone's private joke, a cigarette card of a pin-up girl called Mitzi d'Atti on the back of which someone, perhaps the owner, had written his name, J Summers, followed by a cryptic '39'.

Meanwhile, the Exchange decided to get back into its own building by April 1993, before the anniversary of the bomb. Walter Lilly, this time with architects Rolfe Judd, worked long hours seven days a week to meet the stipulated date for office staff to reoccupy the parts of the ground floor, lower ground and basement at St Mary Axe which were structurally undamaged, and to open the trading Floor in the Queen's Room.

The cost was £650,000. In addition a total of some £3.7 million had been spent by 31 March of that year on preliminary work, demolition and clearance, as well as £1 million for the temporary accommodation at Lloyd's. The new restored areas were opened on 5 April by the Earl of

Caithness, then Minister for Aviation and Shipping. His presence was a reminder of the value which the government places on the contribution which the Baltic Exchange makes to Britain's economy. 'Merchant shipping', he acknowledged, 'not only makes a major contribution towards the creation of national wealth; it also plays an essential role in supporting the UK's defence capability. The Government continually measures the size and state of the merchant fleet against our ever changing defence requirements.' More than 90 per cent by volume of Britain's imports and exports travelled by sea. In 1992 the maritime industries taken together contributed an estimated £4 billion to £5 billion towards the UK's invisible earnings from abroad.

> Wider benefits also flow from the UK's central position as a provider of ancillary shipping services, including of course those offered by the Baltic Exchange itself. These services contribute much to the overall well-being of the City of London. The Government has a general responsibility to foster conditions in which business can flourish, relieved of unnecessary regulatory burdens and free from market-distorting restrictions on international trade.

Invisible earnings for the UK generated by Baltic members in 1992 amounted to US $¾ billion or just over £400 million.

Destruction of the stone and marble of what the *Magazine of Commerce* called 'the veritable fairy palace', where members found customers for their services, was irrelevant. It could not hinder, let alone stop, the world demand for raw materials that generated both the need for bulk shipping and the brokers to negotiate it. Time was when most of it had been done in British ships – 19 million tons gross in 1954 which rose to 24 million (3,858 ships) in 1969; and the British Commonwealth taken altogether accounted for 33 million tons at a time when the US merchant fleet consisted of 19.5 million tons (3,146 ships). When countries round the world were unable to communicate easily and swiftly with each other, and Britain ruled the waves with the world's largest merchant fleet, the United King-dom – and London where all the trading houses were – was domin-ant. Although, with the break-up of the British Empire and with nations everywhere bent on self-determination, London's control weakened, the amount of cargo to be moved increased. More grain had to be shipped to the steadily growing world population, more steel for construction, more coal to generate electricity. Nothing could stop the spread of more sophisticated, more

The severely damaged façade (top right) early on Saturday morning, 11 April 1992, before scaffolding hid it from view. Thirty per cent of the granite was destroyed and only a few Portland stone blocks survived without damage. Even the foundation stone had to be removed from the site (below right).

John Duggan of John Duggan & Co. Ltd, who kept his own photographic record from 11 April 1992 onwards. His albums are displayed on the Floor of the Exchange.

'civilised' lifestyles which demanded the importation of merchandise in which hitherto unsophisticated communities, however successful in achieving political self-determination, were never likely to be self-sufficient. The world's tramp shipping community saw the new world order as very much to their advantage. Though less of the international sea-borne carrying trade was done in British tramp ships, Britain's Baltic Exchange was best placed to make sure that most was made of that advantage and to give the newcomers of the Third World of their experience in providing a service in which two centuries in the business had made them adept.

The accumulation of the skills required to serve tramp shipping interests, whatever the nationality of the principals, learned in the days when London was dominant, has never been dispersed. What has disappeared is the trade in imported grain which thrived on the Baltic through the government's policy of imperial preference, the mainspring of the Australian and Canadian grain and sugar chartering which made so many Baltic brokers prosperous in the

early days of the new Exchange at St Mary Axe. The grain trade, as conducted on the Baltic, faded as trading quantities became larger, more transactions were based on governmental business – particularly to the old USSR – and also as a result of many of the major grain houses moving their offices out of London. The main interest for the domestic market is the weekly meeting of Corn Exchange members on the Floor of the Baltic, although sadly actual selling samples of grain are now rarely seen.

Rubble is cleared from the offices of insurance brokers Inbro Citygate.

The Baltic broker of 1994 is mainly a shipbroker, but one who has had to adapt to the change in the type of trade since the 1960s.

Those who, like Peter Harding, had to meet the changes head-on, know how radical they were. Joining Alexander Howden & Company in 1953, and being made a director in 1960, he became a partner of J E Hyde in 1968 and senior partner in 1972. Elected a director of the Baltic in 1969 and again in 1975, he was chairman from 1981 to 1983.

> It was necessary for a dry cargo broker in the fifties and sixties to spend many hours on the Floor of The Baltic every day, including Saturday mornings, in order to cover the market. General cargo ships were able to engage in a wide variety of trades, and it would have been quite impossible to obtain the necessary information on the telephone. In any case, the people who mattered were themselves on The Baltic for a large part of the day. Telephone calls to Liverpool would be punctuated by pips every three minutes to remind you of the expense of trunk calls. Market reports to principals were given by letter. So the Baltic Exchange was your *primary* place of communication, which it is

no longer. That is now your office and your desk. If you leave your desk today you are in danger of missing primary information. Thirty years ago, if you did not go to The Baltic and you sat at your desk all day, you were in danger of losing your primary information.

One element of shipbroking in those days was for the liner companies that were closely associated with the Baltic and called on its services when they needed extra ships. 'You could take a tramp ship from The Baltic in the 1960s and put it on a liner service. You cannot take a 1990s bulk carrier and put it on a liner service, particularly now with containerisation.'

Another change has been the demise of many of the ship and insurance broker companies, some of the directors of which were Lloyd's marine insurance brokers and others Baltic shipbrokers. For instance, the main business expansion this century of Alexander Howden & Company, leading shipowners and shipbrokers in the last, has been in non-marine insurance, which has brought them phenomenal growth.

The link between Lloyd's and the Baltic, once very close, has become more impersonal, with the same characters no longer being in both places. That the relationship, though not as strong as it once was, is still cordial, however, was demonstrated by the way in which the Corporation of Lloyd's swiftly came to the rescue of the stricken Exchange in April 1992 and organised the immediate leasing of surplus floor space at Lime Street.

With regard to that event, Peter Harding has particular praise for the part played by the police under Commander Hugh Moore of the Bishopsgate area anti-terrorist squad, who sadly died in December 1993 shortly after being injured while making an arrest. As a detective chief inspector, Hugh Moore was responsible for the arrest of Frank Dowling, who shot Peter Harding in the neck and nearly killed him when he interrupted an armed raid on a Fenchurch Street jewellers in October

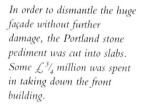

In order to dismantle the huge façade without further damage, the Portland stone pediment was cut into slabs. Some £³/₄ million was spent in taking down the front building.

*Peter Tudball, Lord Mayor
Sir Brian Jenkins and
chairman of Lloyd's David
Coleridge display the rescued
Queen Elizabeth II bell at
Lloyd's in April 1992.*

1971. Dowling and his three accomplices escaped with £43,000 worth of gems and watches. The Baltic Exchange offered £1,000 reward for information leading to the apprehension of the robbers. Three weeks later DCI Moore and his men arrested three of the four. News of the shooting and of Harding's removal to Guy's Hospital at the point of death reached the directors at the board meeting which he should have been attending. They passed a resolution to send round a case of champagne with a note expressing their best wishes for a speedy recovery. At the Old Bailey the following May, Dowling was convicted of attempted murder and sentenced to twenty-one years' imprisonment.

Perhaps the most conspicuous change of the last twenty years has been the greater competition which brokers have to face in 1994. In the 1970s firms were mostly exclusive brokers rather than competitive brokers. The business came to London; the Baltic broker took his business on to the Floor at St Mary Axe; he quoted the Baltic community who disseminated the orders to shipowners or charterers for whom they were acting all over the world. The skill of the Baltic broker then was knowing the right people to contact when a ship was looking for cargo, how to find out what 'off-market' private and confidential business could be picked up. If it was a weak market, with too many empty ships around, shipowners would be reluctant to reveal their 'open' ships. By revealing too much they would give charterers the idea that there were too many ships lying empty and seeking cargoes – which was the case, but was not one to be bruited abroad. If a charterer, on the other hand, had two or three cargoes to be carried, he would only slip one on the market and keep the other two up his sleeve – which was finessing of a kind in which everyone indulged. The place where the bluff could be called was face-to-face on the Floor of the Baltic Exchange.

Beating the competition in 1994 is a matter of getting the information more quickly than the other man. If you are a competitive broker, and several of you have the same order, the one with the best information system will get that order out first and quickest. The slowest way would be to do it via the Floor of the Baltic. The shipowner will take the cargo from the broker who offers it to him first. All will be the same price in the end, as they will all be quoting the same business; the freight rate will be the same whichever channel the shipowner chooses.

With a charterer at one end and a shipowner at the other, the brokers in the middle are only the conduit for the negotiations. They will probably try to guide their principal, but as brokers they do not make the decisions. A shipowner with three brokers coming to him with the same cargo will almost certainly go back to the one that came to him first.

In 'the old days', if a firm received an order from, say, South America, they would have gone to the Baltic Exchange, given the information to those they saw on the Floor and told them to 'cover the market'; and they would have gone running around trying to find a ship. Now, brokers have to go running round, but not round the Floor. There is competition from other centres; they have to go direct to Norway and Germany, to Australia, Japan, Hong Kong and so on. That goes for a charterer's broker looking for a suitable ship to carry his principal's cargo, or a shipowner's broker looking for suitable cargo that his principal's ship can carry. The broker might have a competitive ship or a competitive cargo – that is, a ship or cargo that is not exclusively theirs but open to bids from 'the competition', other brokers seeking such competitive business.

In 1994, because competition has increased, a firm has to do business on a very much wider scale. No longer does everyone do their business in London and through one London broker. The broker's principal may quote a broker in New York and another in Hong Kong, which they would never have done twenty years ago. With them quoting direct into his markets, he has to quote direct as well.

The London-based broker, canvassing the market to find the vessel most suited to carry his principal's dry cargo from A to B, knows relatively quickly the whereabouts of all the ships capable of carrying that volume, and kind, of cargo between the loading and discharging points his principal has specified. To the unacquainted the tramping scene may seem somewhat hit and miss, but as Alan Bloomfield, director of the Dry Cargo Division of H Clarkson & Co. Ltd, explains, it is not as strange as it sounds.

> For instance, an ore charterer could enter the market quoting a cargo of 60,000 tons iron ore from Brazil to Japan for, say, 1/15 January. It is conceivable that ten to 15 ships could make that position. Provided I can negotiate a mutually agreed freight rate for this cargo with the shipowner, the vessel could sail, say, from Rotterdam in ballast to load it. However, before fixing this cargo the shipowner would ask himself if he could use this vessel more profitably – sail to the US Gulf and fix grain to Japan, or proceed to the coal terminals at Hampton Roads on the United States East Coast and load for Europe or Japan.

If he felt the market was improving, the owner could sail to the United States in ballast and take his chances that it would continue to improve and he could obtain a higher rate by presenting his vessel in an ideal position for a potential charterer. It takes about sixteen days to ballast from Rotterdam to the US Gulf, or ten to twelve days to the US east coast. During this period the owner's broker in London will be 'working the market' to find the most profitable fixture for the vessel, which might be costing him around $5,000 to $6,000 a day for crew costs, insurance and the rest, whether idle in Rotterdam, or at sea a further $3,000 a day for ballasting across the Atlantic to the US Gulf.

> This is the essence of Tramp Shipping. There could be around 20 to 30 ships of 60,000 tons dwt – the so-called 'Panamax' size – discharging on the continent of Europe available between September 15 and 30, all seeking their next employment. In the same way grain, coal and other charterers will be canvassing the market seeking tonnage to load their cargoes – grain from US Gulf to Europe or Japan, coal to Europe for delivery between October 1 and 15, a position which would suit these vessels assuming they ballasted from Europe. The London-based broker can ascertain the full spectrum of what is available and play the market to establish the best paying cargo.

For the most part the most profitable cargo is determined by the law of supply and demand. Occasionally a potential charterer enters the market for an early ship, a 'spot' ship. He has learned that a vessel, just arrived in Rotterdam, will be free within the next forty-eight to seventy-two hours, and he will establish, through other brokers, whether this vessel will suit his 'spot' position. He may be told it could be arranged if he is prepared to pay a freight well above the current market level – the 'going rate'. If he needs to move this cargo, he may well concede a higher rate. On the other hand, if the shipowner ballasts to the US Gulf 'unfixed', and the market is falling in the interim, he may have to concede a considerable discount against the previous fixture for the same type of business.

In broad terms, says Alan Bloomfield:

> it is simply a matter of Supply and Demand. Two cargoes and one ship gives the owner the opportunity to command a premium. Conversely, two ships and one cargo could create competition between the owners which may benefit the charterer with a lower freight. With modern communication between all concerned in the shipping business, more and more fixtures are concluded without a signed document, the charter-party. As a general rule, cargoes are delivered and freights paid without problem. How many industries would or could operate on this business? This truly epitomises the motto of The Baltic Exchange, 'Our Word Our Bond'.

In 1994, however, dry cargo is probably the smallest by value of the three types of business done on the Baltic Exchange, and the only one for which brokers habitually use the Floor.

The capacity of the world's merchant fleet is roughly 600 million tons. Half of that is taken up by tankers, and half of their chartering is done by members of the Baltic in London, though without recourse to the Floor. About a third of the world's fleet tonnage is in bulk carriers of dry cargo,

H Clarkson & Co. Ltd, the largest shipbroking company in the world and a leading Baltic member, uses sophisticated information technology to maintain world-wide contacts.

the comparatively new type of vessel designed to carry anything apart from oil, though many of their owners refuse to take iron ore in them. Shipyards have stopped building ore carriers (with maybe less cubic capacity) for heavy ore because they were not flexible enough. There is, however, more demand for the sea-borne carriage of iron ore than for any other dry cargo, and in 1994 much of it is moved in the big Cape size bulk carriers of at least 100,000 tons continually making voyages to the Far East, to and from China and Java, Japan and Korea.

World fleet tonnage for all dry cargo amounts to 200 million tons, a third of the total. The fixing of less than a half of this is done in London. The sixth part of world tonnage (100 million tons) is devoted to liner cargo vessels and container ships which trade on regular services, mainly fixed in Hamburg.

More than half the world's sale and purchase (S & P) business is done in London.

Thus London domination prevails in tanker chartering and S & P, the business of which is conducted by Baltic members, though not on the Exchange Floor. But as a recent chairman of the Baltic Exchange has contended, 'You don't have to have an active Baltic floor to have an active chartering market or an active S & P market. Tanker chartering and Sale & Purchase is more London dominated than dry cargo chartering. London is a big force in dry cargoes but not *the* centre it once was, when *everybody* had to do their business through London.'

And most of it was done personally by the principals of the shipowning companies and of the chartering companies with the principal members of the brokering companies. Few principals of either kind are to be seen on the Floor of the Baltic Exchange in 1994. This does not reflect owner principals' lack of interest in their affairs. It indicates, on the contrary, a shift to their taking greater interest than ever before. A big change seen by Derek Walker in the years between his taking over from his father as secretary of the Baltic Exchange in 1968 and his retirement twenty-four years later was:

> whereas in the past an owner trusted his broker to effect a piece of business, retaining final control, virtually telling him to proceed within limits – it helped if they knew each other, which they did – that ceased being done as much as it used to be. For new circumstances arose, in which an owner could actually control the business and be communicated with more easily. Even if he is on his yacht in the Mediterranean, he can be spoken to by radio telephone. It is a great inducement for people to do the business themselves if they are so inclined. The entrepreneurial shipowners of the latter part of the 20th century have been very much people who have wanted to maintain hands-on control of their own businesses.

A broker with an order in his hand, given a certain amount of time to effect it, used to go to the Exchange, negotiate with people and do the business within the 'authority' which his principal had given him. If he had not got that authority, it meant the shipowner was in control and his agent, the broker, would have to refer back to him. When that was the case, they both had to go to a telephone to give and receive instructions. It was difficult in such circumstances to maintain hands-on control and few attempted it. Those that did had to come to their office, to go to London, and to call at St Mary Axe personally. But with easier access to a telephone, and one that could be relied upon to establish instant communication to any part of the world, it became rarer for a man who had substantial control over business to come onto the Floor.

Traditionally S & P business has always been done directly by the shipowner himself, and from his office. But there are members of the sale and purchase departments of member companies of the Baltic who formed the habit of visiting the Floor at the start of their working life and still think it worthwhile. When he started on the Baltic in 1960, Frank Cordell of Galbraith's was one of thirty or forty young men of his generation who met in the coffee room at St Mary Axe every day for an informal chat. More senior S & P brokers met in the bar; the younger ones in the coffee room.

> All those I met with in the 1960s are still my friends; I still keep up a relationship with them. London is unique in that competitive brokers talk with one another. If you go to any other centre, to be invited to a party, or to be in the presence of another broker, was not The Thing, just not done. Greek S & P brokers have an association, but they don't

meet in the same spirit that we do here. There used to be a London association of S & P brokers operating up to six years ago but we could not get the support of everyone, and it is now inside the Institute of Chartered Shipbrokers.

When his office was near St Mary Axe he went to the Exchange two or three times a week but, now that Galbraith's are south of the river off Tooley Street, he goes there about once a month.

> Buying and selling ships is more leisurely than chartering, but you still have to get to know people. Very few S & P people actually go on the Floor. I may be one of a handful who do. I have some of my clients on The Baltic, so I take the opportunity to see them and maybe have lunch with Dry Cargo brokers I know. I meet people there I would not necessarily speak to on the telephone. It is background you find on the Floor; you don't go there to buy a ship or sell one, but to get information, to find out what is happening, to bump into your clients and discover what they are doing. I enjoy going there, and I think it is an important aspect of my business. It is difficult to do business on the phone within London if people don't know you.

Neil Rokison, another young S & P broker at Galbraith's, realises that the Baltic is less important for S & P than for dry cargo chartering, but sees the benefits from going on the Floor as long term. It gives him the opportunity to meet contemporaries who may be chartering brokers in 1994 but, who knows, may have become S & P brokers or owners' representatives by 2004.

> We will grow up together. People of my age will be managing directors in 15 years' time. The earlier you befriend them, the longer you know them, the more beneficial is it to you. You can talk to people on the phone and send them faxes, but you do not really ever trust them or they trust you fully until you have met them. You can never meet enough people.

S & P brokers are also facing more competition. There are more of them throughout the world, so there is less business for each. Every day there are lists of ships for sale outside London – in Oslo, New York, Hong Kong, Singapore, Piraeus. More S & P business is now done direct between six or seven big centres and many more smaller ones, by-passing London.

However, the shipowner with a broker in London is able to make direct contact through him with potential purchasers anywhere in the world. Those in the market for buying ships expect to be telephoned from London direct. On the other hand, a broker anywhere other than in London has traditionally rarely ventured outside his own domestic market and tends not to get the support of overseas owners that the London brokers have commanded. London S & P brokers have this great advantage over their competitors in other parts of the world. As a result, on average some 50 per cent of all ship sales in the world are arranged through a London-based broker.

Neil Rokison's telephone calls from London are no longer automatically to the broker of the shipowner wanting to sell or buy.

Computerisation makes it very easy to discover who owns what ship. It is easy for any broker to find a ship that is owned by someone in Egypt, say. They have a directory which gives his telephone number and they can try and call him direct. The days are long gone when, discovering the ship was owned by an Egyptian, they felt obliged to phone his broker in Egypt. Everyone can now try to speak directly to *owners* anywhere in the world, and not via his agent. There is very much less inter-broker cooperation in S & P than there used to be.

Some owners who are putting a ship up for sale will insist that a would-be purchaser goes through their broker; but there are others who want to keep commission payments to a minimum and deal with the least number of brokers in the chain that they need to. Twenty years ago an S & P broker automatically associated a shipowner with his broker; he saw the two as working together hand-in-hand. In 1994 that is no longer the case. The S & P member of the Baltic Exchange in London will know the name and location of the owner's broker, but will not necessarily choose to do his business through him.

This being said, more often than not there are two brokers involved in most transactions, one representing the buyer and one the seller, and inter-broker cooperation and good relationships are essential to an S & P broker. Most traditional owners maintain their established broking channels and will only deal through them. It is more the new and expanding companies and countries that are receptive to direct contact and reduced commissions.

To enable people involved in international shipbroking to keep abreast of developments, Galbraith's hold a two-week shipping course every summer at Ashridge Management College. Started thirty-three years ago as a training seminar for their own staff, it is now attended by the experienced employees and brokers of clients – shipowners and trading houses – from all over the world. Galbraith's is the only shipbroking firm to run such a course.

Fax and Telex, and the up-graded long-distance telephone, are only three of the means of doing business which have taken over from meeting, talking and being handed written notices on the Floor of the Baltic Exchange, which was only a walk away from the office, and which was the only human source of business and primary information. Speed, then as now, was of the essence, and the quickest way of fixing a ship was to go and get the order at St Mary Axe. To keep in touch with his office while he was there, a broker had the GPO lay a private telephone line to it from a separate switchboard at the Baltic, monitored by Exchange staff who shouted out the name of the member being called. That system was replaced in the 1970s by a circuit which linked all the telephones on the Floor and elsewhere in the building, all working to a private switchboard. Members could speak to any other member directly by dialling his number on this internal network. This was the system which operated until it was destroyed by the IRA bomb.

Information technology buffs straining to devise speedier systems came up with electronic data processing in the 1960s, but it did not seem to make sense to organise visual display units on the Floor for members who were only going to be there for an hour or two at the most. It was a problem that Derek Walker faced as secretary in the 1970s.

> In their offices members only had their own back-up intelligence system, their own records on principals and broker connections, from which they formulated and acted on their plans and projects. So, if you were to have a comprehensive system, it was essential that the base was as close as possible to where members were working – members who went out of their offices in the early days four or five hours a day and latterly for only two hours or less. The only form that could take would be a super-electronic central dispenser of information so you could bring everyone into the one place, and they would all have the same level of advantage from it, as well as having their own back-up in a branch office near to the central source of information – on the Lloyd's principle of a huge floor or tiers of floors where each unit had its domestic back-up gathered in on a stand, an off-shoot of the main office but still receiving all the information.

With the bewildering pace of technological innovation, what were once problems no longer need solving. The service which seemed desirable but unattainable is replaced by an entirely new way of doing things. To talk of 'telephones', warned American technology consultant George Gilder in *The Economist* supplement 'The Future Surveyed' of 11 September 1993, reflected a lexicographic lag that prevented many business leaders from detecting the onset of *rigor mortis* in their still-profitable products. 'In coming years the very words will ring as quaintly as "horse carriage", "icebox" or "picture radio" today.'

The hand-held cordless mobile telephone has doubtless postponed the death of telephony by a year or two, but Gilder believes the analogue version can only survive if it transforms itself into a digital computer network which functions both over wires and in the air.

> Indeed the most common personal computer of the next decade will be based on the digital cellular telephone. Called Personal Digital Assistants, they will be portable as a watch and as personal as a wallet. They will recognise speech and navigate streets, open the door and start the car, collect the mail and the news and the pay-cheque, connecting to thousands of databases of all kinds.

It is the database connection that interests the Baltic broker. Maybe by the year 2000 his desk will have been replaced by his wrist. Already three major technological developments have transformed telecommunications: computers, super high frequency radio via an orbiting satellite radio repeater in the ionosphere, and fibre optics – and these, together with the submarine cable (the first was laid between Dover and Calais in 1851), are certain to dominate the future of the world's telecommunications systems, on which members of the Baltic rely. Computers allow them to manage, control and store traffic; the others give the channel capacity to accommodate the predicted traffic growth. General telephone traffic is expected to continue increasing at 20 per cent a year to 2000 and beyond. The biggest growth is anticipated in man-to-machine and machine-to-machine links, with digital data flow forming the bulk of the traffic. High speed digital facsimile is in the offing, with machines that can already transmit A4-sized documents in twenty seconds. And then there are the Windows-compatible corporate databases; 'Twin Peeks' technology which equips a personal computer with a camera through which one can see other computer users, working on a telephone line; the pen-based portable computer, electronic book or 'Personal Communicator'; a system called 'Groupware' which turns a personal computer into a team one, bringing together groups of people sitting in different offices in the same building with people in another town, in another country, enabling them to work together as if they were in the same room.

> The new networks will move vastly more data in both directions. They can tie together parts of businesses, sending spectacularly lifelike designs from Detroit to machine shops in Manila. And a network is more than links between places; it is itself a place. People round the world use the Internet, the planet's biggest computer network, to talk about everything from Zoroastrianism to astrophysics. Nobody yet knows what else 'the Net' will be used for as the universe behind the screens expands. (*The Economist*, 16 October 1993)

And maybe, even before 2000, the 'place' that is the Net will have taken the place of the Floor – though a glass screen can never replace a club.

SIX

LONDON RULES THE WAVES

for traders and shipowners

There is only time to master one technique before the backroom boys invent another which they claim will be superior, and all must assimilate, if they are to stay in the race to be the first with the offer, let alone win it. It is no new experience, however, for members of the Baltic Exchange who manage or own merchant shipping fleets, whose role is shipbroker, shipping agent, trading house, port authority or legal adviser, to have to adjust to changing means of transport and communication, to a changing political and commercial scene. Never before, however, have they had to do that so frequently.

The histories of member companies who started in business one hundred or two hundred years ago, many of whom are active in 1994, illustrate how they have reorganised their management style to accommodate the replacement of sail by steam, of the horse-drawn carriage by the automobile, of the mail coach by the train and telegraph, to serve new markets and new nations.

North Shields master mariners Ralph and Robert Clarke, who by purchasing an interest in the 300-ton sailing vessel *Cleveland* engaged in the North American trade in 1730, laid the foundation of the business which in 1994 is Baltic member Stephenson Clarke Shipping Ltd of Newcastle upon Tyne, shipowners and ship managers. They would have waited several days for letters from London where in 1775 Robert's son John (by his wife Jane Stephenson) acted as agent for his father and uncle. Joined by his brother Ralph, the firm – with offices in the Coal Exchange at Billingsgate – were mainly coal factors, but by 1805 were styling themselves 'coal factors, shipping and insurance brokers'. From 1850, as Stephenson Clarke & Company with offices in St Dunstans Alley, they built up a fleet of the steam colliers which had supplanted the small 'Geordie Brig' sailing craft that carried coal on a regular liner service from the north to the London River and south coast. They were the forerunners of the specialised bulk carriers designed to handle one cargo in one trade, a type that developed into the 1980s coal carrier, ore or sugar carrier and oil tanker.

In 1912 Stephenson Clarke became managers of the Gas Light & Coke Company's first steam collier, and three years later they began a long working association with the Powell Duffryn Steam Coal Company, which in 1928 acquired the whole of their ordinary share capital. Through Powell Duffryn, in 1970 they bought the fleet of William Robertson established in Glasgow in 1852; in 1975 they added two 12,000-ton bulk carriers to their fleet of small coastal colliers, tankers, workhorse hopper barges and romantic 'flatties'. The next year they formed Powell Duffryn Shipping Services Ltd to handle, separately from their shipowning interests, brokerage, sale and purchase, and ship chartering services.

For David Watkins, managing director of the 264-year-old sizeable operation that is the Stephenson Clarke Shipping business of 1994, belonging to the 'club', which was formed fourteen years after their foundation, is greatly valued. As his predecessor as managing director, Grahame Stafford, wrote in his foreword to *A Link with Tradition*, marking the company's 250th anniversary in 1980:

> I believe our success could not have been achieved without the friendship and support of our many business friends, and would like to say how much we appreciate the close associations we have with our customers and those who provide us with the services essential to our operations.

Cory Brothers Shipping Ltd of Tilbury Docks trace their origins back to the leading firm in the London coal trade of William Cory & Son, founded in 1785. They soon began handling oil as well, and from the beginning of the oil era were the sole general bunker sales agent to the BP Trading Company for the bunkering of ships throughout the world. They acquired three 19,000-ton ocean-going tankers and four 15,000-ton ore carriers. In 1896 they amalgamated the majority of their vessels into a single fleet owned by William Cory & Son Ltd.

The business of Baltic member Scrutton Son & Company started with the marriage in 1793 of stockbroker James Scrutton with the daughter of the master of a sailing ship plying the West Indies trade. When James died in 1804 when he was only 37, his son Thomas Scrutton set up as owner and manager of vessels, mainly with homeward shipment of sugar, rum, coffee and slaves from Jamaica to New Orleans, but also trading to the Mediterranean, America and India. The only way the ships' masters could communicate with England was to give a message to a passing ship which would arrive home before them. His descendants, who were owning twenty-two ships by 1874, had a fleet of nine steamers ten years later, which could do four round trips a year instead of one. The brothers James and Frederic Scrutton became representative members of the Baltic in 1892, the year after they formed the Direct Line Shipping Company trading to the West Indies and Belize, by which time there was an efficient network of submarine telegraph cables linking the Caribbean and South America with England.

The germ of the international operation of P & O Containers, P & O

Stephenson Clarke's Washington *at sea.*

Right: Emerald, *one of seven vessels recalling Gem Line Ltd, which became part of Stephenson Clarke in 1978.*

Bulk Carriers and P & O Tankships was Shetlander Arthur Anderson joining the London office of shipbroker Brodie McGhie Willcox in 1815 and seven years later becoming a partner. The two of them swiftly built up links with the Iberian peninsula. During the Portuguese and Spanish civil wars of the early 1830s they supported the legitimate heirs to both thrones, and in 1835 they joined Captain Richard Bourne, a Dublin shipowner, in establishing a regular service between London, Spain, Portugal and Gibraltar under the name of the Peninsular Steam Navigation Company. Financial security came in 1837 with their winning a contract to carry mails between Falmouth, Vigo, Oporto, Lisbon, Cadiz and Gibraltar. Another for a mail run to Alexandria followed in 1840, and they were able to raise £1 million to form a limited liability company,

ULLSWATER
HONG KONG

the Peninsular and Oriental Steam Navigation Company was incorporated by royal charter, under which it still trades, being one of the few British companies in 1994 not operating under the Companies Acts.

Also part of P & O Containers Ltd is H E Moss & Co. Ltd. Its founder, Henry Moss, began business in Liverpool in 1827. By 1854 his company was operating as coal merchant, colliery agent, insurance broker, bill broker and shipbroker. A London office was opened in 1860 at 83 Fenchurch Street. The business prospered, and in 1889 the first of a sizeable fleet of product carriers, the tanker *Lumen*, was ordered. In 1964 H E Moss & Co. Ltd, now purely shipowner, shipbroker and ship agent, was bought by the Cunard Steam-ship Co. Ltd and the head office moved to London. As part of Cunard Cargo Shipping, it was bought by P&O Containers Ltd in 1991.

In the same way that Arthur Anderson entered the shipowning scene via a London shipbroker, in 1869 two 21-year-old cousins, Reginald Turnbull and Robert Scott, came south to London from the ancient port of Whitby on the River Esk to join a shipbroking firm. Reginald's father had become a partner with his father, trading as Thomas Turnbull & Son, in 1840. They owned sailing ships on the sixty-fourth share system, and then steamships, and they offered dry dock and repair facilities. Reginald, Thomas's third son, and Robert, the son of his sister Ann who had married Archibald Scott, had already done a certain amount of shipbroking and ship chartering work at Whitby. But Thomas Turnbull & Son realised that to operate a steam tramp ship profitably they would have to change their management style. As Anne and Russell Long point out in their centenary history of Turnbull's from 1872 to 1972, *A Shipping Venture*, voyage estimates could now be accurately worked out with the passage time at sea being a known quantity, rather than the mystical figure it was for a sailing vessel dependent on wind, weather, tide and ocean currents. Because of the preference of London bankers for financing the old and well-established liner companies, and their regarding the small and often underpowered tramp ship as a speculative risk, there was a concentration of steam tramp shipowners on the north-east coast of England – and in Cardiff to serve the South Wales coal industry.

Before the connection of Whitby to the telegraph system, all communication between Thomas Turnbull & Son and their brokers, including the negotiation of charter-parties, was conducted by letters delivered either by hand or through the post. Homeward freights outside the brokers' sphere of operations abroad were arranged by the master empowered by his owners, co-owners or managers to negotiate the rate of freight and the terms and conditions of the relevant charter-party on the spot. With the creation of an inland electric telegraph system and a world-wide submarine telegraph cable system, the shipbroker's ability to serve shipowners in the coverage of freight markets locally and overseas was revolutionised. Thomas Turnbull realised that in these circumstances it was essential to have a presence in London, the world's commercial centre, and 'having been blessed with numerous children he rightly considered that the most expedient way of doing this and, as a wily Yorkshireman, the cheapest, was to set up his male offspring accordingly'.

After three years' gaining experience in another's office, in 1872 Reginald Turnbull and Robert Scott registered themselves in a joint partnership as Turnbull, Scott & Company, ship and insurance brokers,

P & O's Ullswater *at sea with a 100,000-tonne cargo.*

Thomas Turnbull's first vessel, Alpha, *which was launched from Larpool in 1840.*

with an office in Gracechurch Street. A first priority of the two partners was to be elected members of the Baltic, which they duly secured two months after opening for business. From the telegraph office at St Mary Axe they sent any urgent messages to Whitby, particularly firm offers, as well as market information complementing their negotiations. Every day they posted a letter to Whitby giving written confirmation of any negotiations, a general report of market conditions and details of all the business they had done that day.

> This procedure, once adopted, became a standard daily practice, and if the letter was not received, Whitby would telegraph to London 'Your letter not received', indicating how important constant market information was to the Turnbulls in Whitby for the operation of their fleet and for vessels of other owner friends who made use of the excellent broking service being offered by the company. (*A Shipping Venture*)

Turnbull, Scott & Company carried on their business in London for ninety-nine years until 1970 when they moved out to Farnborough – 'with modern methods in communication it was felt that the necessity of being situated in the heart of the City no longer existed'. The routine work could be carried on as successfully in Farnborough as in London, with reduced overheads and no commuting. Two years later, with M T (Tommy) Turnbull vice-chairman of the Baltic (he was chairman from 1973 to 1975), the firm celebrated their centenary, and in 1986 Tommy was made an honorary member. In 1994, however, Turnbull Scott no longer own any ships; they sold their last one early in 1991 and gave up their chartering business shortly afterwards. Having to find vast sums in interest payments on bank loans, and having to pay up to £2,000 a day to lay a ship up, most small fleet owners in Britain have found that shipowning has become too capital intensive for them – but not all.

Frederick Everard was the foreman shipwright at Keep's barge yard at Greenhithe on the Thames, and in 1880 he became yard manager, and then its owner. He soon had a busy life building and repairing traditional spritsail barges of the London river. When one year he took a barge in payment of a bad debt, he became an instant shipowner. In 1895 he made a more orthodox purchase of the barge *Elizabeth*, which had been abandoned by its owner after it had sunk in a collision six years previously and had been raised by the Thames Conservancy Board, who was the vendor. He added to his 'fleet' with the purchase in 1906 of three sailing barges built in Sweden and by building for himself, ten years later, the motor vessel *Grit*. He specialised in carrying cement to builders' yards; delivering coal to gasworks; and grain and cattlefeed, bricks and stone, china clay and roadstone up and down the coast. In the 1950s he was shipping coal, timber and pulp further afield, to the Baltic Sea.

Everard of Greenhithe, which Frederick Everard formed in 1922 on the same Greenhithe site, bought thirty-six tankers between 1945 and 1957 from 180 dwt to 5,127 dwt; and they diversified into shipbuilding and repairing at Yarmouth, oil storage and transport services. They bought quarries in Devon, and wharfage and warehousing in Plymouth; and in 1962 they bought Matthews & Luff, a shipbroking firm established in 1845, which was absorbed into Everard's chartering department (wound up in 1985). Purchases after 1961 included Glen & Company of Glasgow, T Salvesen & Company, David Traill & Sons of Grangemouth, and Urban Korner AJB of Gothenburg. In the 1960s Everard's had built twenty-two vessels and bought another twelve. In 1994 the family still own and manage what is now F T Everard & Sons Ltd, of which F M Everard CBE is chairman. They have long been Baltic members and their registered office is where the enterprise began, in Greenhithe.

When in 1980 they celebrated the centenary of Frederick Everard's purchase of Keep's Yard, Greenhithe, they had just bought Comben Longstaffe & Company, and became active in ship management. Eight years later, however, they closed the shipyard at Greenhithe and demolished it. They were now full-time shipowners. They bought a couple of Japanese tankers and in 1989 they formed Short Sea Europe PLC. The names they gave their tankers reflected the secret of their survival – *Alacrity, Assiduity, Amity, Authority, Agility*. The master of the last named, Captain Keith Reading, told David Harrison of the *Observer* that with the British merchant fleet reaching the point of no return, if the decline went on it would soon be too late to build it up again. 'All those skills developed over the centuries will just disappear.' Britain no longer had enough merchant ships, he said, to provide the level of support given to HM Forces in the Falklands.

Such as were mustered then – and there were in fact a good number – were mostly requisitioned by the government through the Baltic and the government's freight market representative for the Department of Transport. At the time of the campaign mounted in 1983 to retake the Falkland Islands after Argentina's invasion, known as Operation

Corporate, the representative was John Maccoy, originally of Birt Potter & Hughes, who had been acting as such since 1968.

The government first nominated a representative to charter merchant ships on its behalf in 1942 in the middle of World War 2. This was Baltic member Sir John Gibson Graham of Galbraith Pembroke & Company who represented the Ministry of War Transport until the war ended in 1945. He was succeeded as freight market representative to what had become the Ministry of Transport by Herbert Roberts, who was followed in 1959 by Cyril Warwick. When John Maccoy retired in 1986 the post, although still an honorary appointment by the government, was taken over by the Baltic. Richard Bilton undertook the work for the Exchange as a member of the staff, and chartered many roll-on roll-off ferries and cargo ships for the Ministry of Defence for use in Operation Granby, the British and US operation to liberate Kuwait after the Iraqi invasion in 1990. The Exchange receives a commission only for the charters arranged for defence work and for other government departments. Other activities of the freight market representative at that time included the charter and eventual sale to the Ministry of Defence of a replacement for HMS *Endurance*, the Antarctic ice patrol ship, together with many miscellaneous charters of tugs, heavy lift and survey ships. When the United Nations sent in a protection and relief force to Bosnia in the Balkans – Operation Grapple – Richard Bilton was instrumental in arranging many of the charters for commercial shipping. In August 1993 new arrangements were negotiated with the Ministry of Defence by which the Exchange covered the costs of the freight market representative from a flat fee from the MoD together with a small commission on the value of the charters arranged.

Baltic shipbroking companies are frequently called upon to charter vessels for the world-wide movement of the armed forces of many different countries. One company alone has carried the military forces of Poland, Germany, Britain, Italy, France, Canada, Argentina, Uruguay, India, Pakistan, Bangladesh, China, Japan and Australia to peace-keeping missions in Angola, Namibia, Croatia and Bosnia, Cambodia, Somalia and Mozambique. The work they did for Britain involved the transport of a field hospital unit to Bosnia.

It would have been to support Britain's fighting men in India that any supply ships would have been requisitioned in 1844, a hundred years after the opening of the Virginia and Baltic Coffee House, when 16-year-old Edwin Savory Houlder got himself a job in the London office of Greek merchants Ionides Sgouta & Company. Ships had been needed to victual the troops of Sir Charles Napier who the year before had conquered Sind – and had sent a note to free-trade prime minister Sir Robert Peel bearing the one Latin word *Peccavi* – 'I have sinned'. The Anglo-Sikh War was to break out the following year. There was no serious dislocation of the sea-borne carrying trade, and when Houlder became 21 he was allowed to trade on his own account from Sgouta's office. By 1853 he had so much work on his hands that he took an office of his own in Gracechurch Street and began business as E S Houlder & Company, ship and insurance brokers.

The discovery of gold in New South Wales in 1851 created not only a rush of prospectors but a demand for goods of every description to fuel Australia's new economy. By 1860 Edwin Houlder and his brother Alfred, who joined him in 1856, were chartering and loading on a regular basis

British and American clippers to sail from London to Melbourne. Another brother, Augustus, became a partner in 1867 and the company was renamed Houlder Brothers. Soon they were shipping coal to India and South Africa; in 1881 they started the trade for which they became famous, the carriage of frozen meat. The partnership became a limited liability company in 1898, and the following year they formed Houlder Line Ltd to take over the fleet which had been owned either in sixty-fourth shares or by single ship companies.

The year 1901 saw the beginning of recession, and Edwin Houlder collapsed and died at the firm's annual general meeting of that year when shareholders had criticised the results and the management. Edwin's son Frank Houlder, a Baltic member since 1890, became chairman. In 1911 Houlder Brothers & Company sold a 50 per cent interest in their business to Furness Withy & Company, which had been founded in 1891 in Hartlepool in north-east England when Christopher Furness merged his business interests with those of Edward Withy, a shipbuilder from nearby West Hartlepool. Houlder Brothers continued to play an independent role, however. Christopher Furness had been a partner with his brother in Thomas Furness & Company, which had traded in foodstuffs since 1878, and operated ships across the Atlantic between Hartlepool and Boston, Massachusetts. In 1870, at the outbreak of the Franco-Prussian War, the 19-year-old Christopher, in Gothenburg where he had been sent to find

Sir Christopher Furness (1852–1912) who – together with Edward Withy – founded Furness, Withy & Company in Hartlepool in 1891.

cheaper supplies of grain, had no means of telling his father in Hartlepool about Swedish corn and the number of ships lying idle in the port owing to the French blockade of the Elbe. In the absence of any line of communication with England, he had to act upon his own initiative. He bought large quantities of corn, and chartered and despatched ships loaded with it to Hartlepool where the shortage had caused prices to rise. The venture netted £55,000 which – as the chairman of Furness Withy in their centenary year 1991, J E Keville, observed – was the price of building two 3,000-ton steamers. 'What 19-year-old today would be given such authority!'

Many famous shipping companies passed into Furness Withy control apart from Houlder Brothers: notably Royal Mail Lines, the Pacific Steam Navigation, Manchester Liners, Shaw Savill and Albion. In 1980 the company was bought by C Y Tung Group of Hong Kong; in 1987 it moved its head office to Redhill; in 1990 it was sold again to the Hamburg-based Oetker Group. Furness Withy (Chartering), created in 1971, has retained its head office in London, however, and has a subsidiary in Melbourne. In London they act as brokers for both charterers and owners outside the group, and also act as principals operating short-term time-chartered tonnage on a world-wide basis, where that does not conflict with the group's liner interests. Since 1971 the company have witnessed the demise of the long-term cargo contract against which ships were built or bought second-hand. They have also seen a great change in trading patterns as Japan has set up manufacturing plants in several of its mature markets, bringing a change in its shipowning policies and raw material imports. Furness Withy (Chartering) have benefited from bulk shipping, which has enabled them to carry a wider range of semi-finished manufactured goods unsuited to shipment in containers.

One of the nineteenth-century Houlder family branched out in 1885 and founded in his own name the company which today remains independent and is still called Howard Houlder and Partners Ltd. The company concentrates on a core activity of shipbroking. Seventy years ago HHP pioneered the Baltic's relations with Far Eastern principals who dominate many areas from the liner types through car carriers to bulk carriers. HHP have offices in Tokyo and Manila; and joint ventures in Moscow, Plzen and New York to continue the Baltic's links with East and West as well as with Europe.

In the 1920s Howard Houlder left the company he had founded and shortly afterwards formed a new company, Howard Tenens – a deliberate pun on his surname, *tenens* meaning 'holding', from the Latin verb *tenere*, to hold. Obviously, as Richard Bilton – who joined Howard Tenens (and became its Baltic representative) in 1957 – commented, Howard Houlder had to choose another name for his new company.

Richard Bilton belongs to one of the several Baltic families who have had members in the Exchange for a century or more. His grandfather Henry Turner, of grain merchants William H Pim Junior, heads the list. Henry's brother Walter Turner – of another leading grain house, Bunge & Company – became a member at the same time. Henry's eldest son Gordon took over from him as chairman of Pim's. Gordon Turner's eldest son David was the Baltic representative of the Continental Group of grain companies of which Pim's had become a part.

Henry Turner's youngest son R S (Dick) Turner joined Lambert Brothers (now part of Inchcape Shipping Services) after World War 2 service in the Honourable Artillery Company, and remained with the company until his retirement in the mid-1980s. His son Brian Turner worked for some time as a shipbroker in London, and in 1994 was running a broking company in Hong Kong. Henry Turner's daughter was Richard Bilton's mother. After fifteen years with Howard Tenens Ltd, Richard left it in 1972 to start Seabulk Chartering Ltd, from which he moved in 1986 to take over the position of freight market representative to the Department of Transport. His younger brother Philip Bilton worked for various shipbroking companies in Bristol, London and Copenhagen and was a Baltic member from 1961 to 1986.

It is continuity of service to the merchant shipping community – not only in Britain but all over the world – of the kind given by three generations of Turners, and their absorption of the traditions which they take with them to other maritime nations, which contributes so weightily to the authority in the field of merchant shipping for which the Baltic is world renowned.

David Brown styled himself shipbroker and shipowner when at the age of 30 he set up in Leadenhall Street in 1860. Six years later he took on John Bowden as partner, and engaged a clerk called William Jenkinson. By 1877 Jenkinson had become a fully fledged shipbroker and David Brown took him into partnership – they became Brown Jenkinson & Company, shipbrokers. In the 1890s they made ship chartering agreements with Thomas Harling & Company of Liverpool, Carlisle & Company, Thomas Raison & Company, and a firm in Norway. They organised time-charters to New York and Europe in competition with liners. With a new partner, Robert Forster, they built up business with Australia. Forster had left F Lenders & Company, for whom he had been the company's representative on the Baltic for ship chartering. Since they were charterers' brokers and not owners' brokers, they suffered a setback at the outbreak of World War 2, but were soon developing a North Sea trade and acting as UK agents for J A Winchester of New York.

When J S Sutcliffe was appointed chairman of John Sutcliffe & Son (Holdings) of Grimsby in 1988, the year in which the group was reorganised, he was the latest in a long line to head the family firm which John Sutcliffe of Rochdale had founded in 1862. Their appointment of Keith Craig as managing director in the 1970s marked the first time a non-family director was asked to act in an executive capacity. He came from an established Liverpool shipbroking firm with a 100-year-old association with the London Shipping Exchange and the Baltic: Gellatly, Hankey & Company. In 1986 another break was made with family tradition when Christopher Thompson was elected as chairman.

Founder John Sutcliffe began his career in shipping when in 1857 he took the position of shipping agent to the West Hartlepool Steam Navigation Company, established the year before as a subsidiary of the West Hartlepool Harbour and Railway Company with six first-class steamships operating to Hamburg and St Petersburg. When in 1862 the parent company failed, John Sutcliffe, then aged 49, moved to Grimsby as shipping and forwarding agent of the Anglo-French Steamship Company, which had been formed in 1856 by the Manchester, Sheffield and Lincolnshire Railway Company. In the summer of 1862 Anglo-French

asked John Sutcliffe to organise a shipping and forwarding agency for the company, and he formed John Sutcliffe & Company, with offices in Royal Dock Chambers, Grimsby. In a short time the company started acting as general shipping agents and shipbrokers, though the business of Anglo-French was the priority until it was dissolved in 1865. The next year John Sutcliffe & Company were put in charge of all the shipping arrangements of the Manchester, Sheffield and Lincolnshire Railway. When in 1872 John had his son Jack join him in partnership, the firm became John Sutcliffe & Son; and when his father died in 1877, Jack consolidated the company and greatly expanded its activities. John Sutcliffe & Son were run as a partnership until 1936, when John Sutcliffe & Son (Grimsby) Ltd were formed to take over the work done at the port, offer services as shipbrokers and charterers, and act as shipping agents.

Robert Ropner, who in 1874 founded what is now Baltic member Ropner Shipping Services Ltd, came to the north-east from the Continent as an immigrant. Born in Germany in 1838, he emigrated to England when he was 20 and found work in a Hartlepool coal business. In 1860 he moved to T Appleby & Company, a West Hartlepool shipowner, and six years later he went into partnership with them as Appleby, Ropner & Company, which owned eight ships. They split up in 1874, and Ropner took over five of the ships which he ran in the Baltic and China Sea trades. He opened an office in London in 1887, and took his son William into partnership in 1891. He was knighted in 1902 and made a baronet in 1904. By the time Sir Robert Ropner died in 1924 aged 86, his four grandsons, sons of William, had joined the firm. The head office was moved to Darlington in 1946, and the next year the first

Jack Sutcliffe, the son in John Sutcliffe & Son, surrounded by associates on board one of his ships around 1910.

member of the fourth generation of Ropners joined the family firm. Delivery of two 106,490-ton bulk carriers in 1971 marked the beginning of liaison with the Norwegian Bulk Carriers consortium of owners. The writer of the foreword in the booklet published to celebrate their centenary from 1874 to 1974 believed that a very rough calculation revealed that the Ropner fleet, during its 100-year life had carried some 250 million tons of cargo ranging from iron ore to Rolls-Royce motor cars and, on the liquid side, from crude oil to the finest Scotch whisky.

One of those who took shares in R Ropner & Company (who also owned Comben Longstaffe) was Charles Hunting, whose father had purchased two sailing ships in 1874 and set up, with one William Pattison, on Quayside, Newcastle upon Tyne, as 'shipbrokering, ship and steamship owners and managers'. The first ship built for Hunting & Pattison in 1877 traded mainly in European waters. In 1886 Hunting & Pattison opened a London office in Great St Helen Street to do business as ship managers, charterers and brokers as well as shipowners. In 1891, however, the partnership was dissolved. The following year the firm became Hunting & Son which started operating the Hunting fleet's first tank steamship, the *Duffield* – one of the earliest of such ships to be built in Britain. Charles Hunting explored the potential of oil trade with shipbroker Edward Aisbett Gibson, the first tank chartering agent in London. From then on the association between C S Hunting and E A Gibson was very close. In the 1920s the Hunting family took over E A Gibson (Shipbrokers). After the collapse in 1981 of the Seabridge Consortium, of which Huntings had been a founder member in 1968, and their selling their remaining ships along with Hunter Stag Management, the Hunting family's shipowning interests ceased. They diversified into aviation, travel and insurance broking.

Another founder member of the Seabridge Consortium, the Bibby Line, still operating in 1994, originated in Ormskirk to the north of Liverpool, where John Bibby was born in 1775. At the age of 26 he and William Hall formed Bibby & Hall, shipbrokers. Four years later he had acquired another partner, John Highfield, with whom he traded as John Bibby & Company, which was both a shipbroking and a merchanting business. The start of what became the Bibby Line dates from 1807 when John Bibby & Company began organising regular sailings from Liverpool to Dublin, the Baltic Sea and South America, but mainly to the Mediterranean. From 1821 John Bibby was operating on his own, and by the 1830s his company had eighteen vessels with a regular line between Liverpool and Lisbon. Expansion came fast under John's sons James and John, and in the 1850s John Bibby Sons & Company were running steamers to all the Mediterranean ports from Gibraltar to Messina. In 1865 the Bibby fleet consisted of twenty-three modern steamers; and when the Bibby Steamship Company was formed in Liverpool in 1891 it was managed by Bibby Brothers & Company.

The formation of the British bulk carrier pool, the Seabridge Consortium – of which Derek Hall was managing director – in 1968 brought a great deal of business to Baltic shipbrokers. Huntings and Bibbys were joined in this enterprise by H Clarkson & Company, the Bowring Steamship Company, and Houlder Brothers. The Seabridge owners placed orders for many ships, varying in size from 45,000 to 180,000 tons.

One of their vessels, the *Tweed Bridge*, built in the Japanese yard of

Mitsubishi Heavy Industries, was named in April 1974 by Miss Deborah Hunting at a ceremony overseen by a Shinto priest dressed in a white and purple robe, black hat and clogs, who waved a branch of a sacred tree and called upon a deity to bless the ship. With the crisis of 1973, however, world oil consumption declined, and after her maiden voyage the *Tweed Bridge* lay idle for many weeks waiting for her first Australian cargo. Huntings had already ordered a second ship, the *Tyne Bridge*. But these and other ships were sold, and the Seabridge Consortium was disbanded in 1981. The idea of operating ultra large dry bulk carriers, then ore bulk oil (OBO) carriers, on a pooled basis was a sound one but the timing was wrong, which no one could have foreseen.

More lasting was Associated Bulk Carriers (ABC), a company formed in Bermuda in 1963 as a joint venture between P & O Steam Navigation Company and the Anglo Norness Shipping Company to manage their bulk and combination carriers. Anglo Norness, a prominent tanker company, were building up a growing fleet of such bulk carriers – by 1967 they had fifty (more than two million tons) – while P & O were seeking to develop their traditional tramp operations carried out previously by the Hain Steam Ship Company. P & O's first bulk carrier was delivered in 1965, and its first OBO carrier in 1966.

ABC, who generated a considerable amount of work for Baltic Exchange shipbrokers, chartered ships from both P & O and Anglo Norness, and when necessary from outside concerns also. In 1969 the Zapata Group took over Anglo Norness, which was then renamed Zapata Naess Shipping Company. In 1973 P & O and Palmerston Holdings each took a 50 per cent share in Zapata Naess, which they renamed Anglo Nordic Shipping. At the time of the takeover Anglo Nordic and its subsidiaries owned bulk and combination carriers, tankers and chemical carriers – a fleet of twenty-four ships of 2,400,000 dwt. At its peak in 1976 ABC controlled some twenty-six ships of about 3,100,000 dwt. In a promotional brochure of 1967 they said they had developed the design for a ship which allowed them to match bulk cargoes of coal, grain and ore with liquid ones; three of such OBOs were operational and two more were on the way. And they had a device they called 'Trade Route Study':

> We sit down with a charterer and lay our trade routes on the table. He does the same. We match up his cargoes and our movements. In the end we come up with a formula that appeals to us both. It's like taking two poker hands, pooling them and coming up with four aces. It works.

In 1982 ABC became a wholly owned subsidiary of P & O, and two years later they renamed it P & O Bulk Carriers Ltd. Carl Timmerman is the managing director and their head office is in London. In 1994 they conduct the world-wide movement of iron ore, coking coal and steam coal for the world's leading steel producers, power utilities and raw material shippers. Their bulk carriers, ranging in size between 100,000 and 190,000 tonnes, carry some 17 million tonnes of cargo every year. Under the umbrella of P & O Bulk Shipping Ltd, the company also operates, through P & O Tankships Ltd (formerly Rowbotham Tankships), a fleet of clean petroleum product carriers employed predominantly in UK coastal and North European waters.

In 1959 the Chinese government decided to charter vessels to repatriate overseas Chinese from Indonesia. It was a dress rehearsal for the China Ocean Shipping Company (COSCO), founded in 1961, which now has offices in Essex as COSCO (UK) Ltd. Services to Japan and Korea followed in 1964, and in 1975 COSCO's fleet had grown to a total deadweight tonnage in excess of five million tons, a yearly increase of nearly a million tons. COSCO's achievements meant that by 1980 China's tonnage had increased to 9.60 million dwt and dependence on chartered foreign ships for the major part of its foreign trade came to an end.

Ninety sailings a month are made by container vessels to the Persian Gulf, the US east and west coasts, North West Europe, Japan, South East Asia, the Mediterranean Sea, Australia and Hong Kong. COSCO now has over fifty container ships, ranking high in the world's container fleet.

COSCO laid its foundation in the 1950s, made its first step in the 1960s, toddled in the 1970s and marched on confidently in the 1990s after China's adoption of the policy of reform and opening up. Today, now known as China Ocean Shipping Company, it owns and operates more than 620 ships of 15 million dwt.

In the 1990s F T Everard, Andrew Weir, T & J Harrison, P & O, Bibby and Ropner are representatives of the few survivors on the British merchant shipping scene. Graig is the sole remaining Welsh company.

Other surviving names like Denholms of Glasgow had long since diversified into ship management, where they are now one of the world's leading players. Nevertheless, Denholm Coates, the broking arm, retains its Baltic links dating back to 1903. Since 1969 they have been brokers for the Atlantic Bulker Pool of handysize ships, and Tim Brown – the current chairman and a Baltic member since 1954 – serves as a director of the Exchange. In May 1993 Britain's Chamber of Shipping saw the British merchant fleet 'on track to disappear altogether'. British companies still owned enough tonnage to rank eleventh in the world shipping league, but the amount of that shipping registered in the UK put Britain at

Computer screens, Telex and fax dominate the modern shipbroker's office. Here at Simpson, Spence & Young, one of the Baltic's biggest members, the integrated office allowing rapid communication both with others in the broking team and the clients world-wide is shown. Simpson, Spence & Young's wide business covers both wet and dry cargoes, including minerals and grain, and buying and selling ships.

No. 33, less than 0.5 per cent of the world total, compared with 26 per cent in 1939. More than 80 per cent of the UK-owned fleet has abandoned the Red Ensign and switched to a flag of convenience. In October 1993 the House of Commons Select Committee on Employment, in an inquiry into the future of maritime skills and employment in the UK, reported critically on emerging shortages.

MPs and the Labour opposition are not alone in deploring the decline. 'It is a source of some sadness to us', John Hadjipateras, chairman of the Greek Shipping Co-operation Committee, told Deep Singh, editor of *The Baltic* magazine, in June 1992. 'We would like to see a larger British fleet, but the decline was not due to the role of governments but to three factors.' So many shipowning firms became public companies which meant decisions were made by a board of directors – 'shipping simply does not work

like that'. The sons of the major British shipowners chose not to go into shipping. The British trade unions imposed restrictive practices.

A general cargo line ship at sea, with a load of tractors on deck.

> The government may have played a small role, but British shipping had always enjoyed massive subsidies and could not cope with their withdrawal. And of course, the end of the British Empire meant that the new Commonwealth could become major shipping countries in their own right rather than relying on the British fleet.

It was while the British Empire was at its peak, but it and the rest of the world was in the grip of an economic crisis of unprecedented proportions, that the committee of which John Hadjipateras is chairman came into being. As Nicholas Metaxas, its first secretary, related in Andreas Lemos's book *The Greeks and the Sea* (1976), managers of major Greek shipping offices in London met with representatives of the British Maritime Chamber in 1935 to devise means of alleviating the effects of the crisis. The scheme they suggested for the voluntary laying up of a certain part of their tonnage to cope with the oversupply in the freight market was adopted by the British Maritime Chamber, who established the Tramp Shipping Co-operation Committee to carry it out. On their side the Greek shipping offices in London, except for Goulandris Brothers, were organised into a central agency which they called the Greek Shipping Co-operation Office, with Pericles Dracoulis as chairman, Angelo Lusi as vice-chairman and Nicholas Metaxas as secretary (until 1940). In 1937 they took an office at 31 St Mary Axe alongside the Baltic Exchange, and met there once a week.

The mechanically propelled Greek merchant fleet lost some 74 per cent of its ships and 71 per cent of its tonnage during World War 2; it also lost 551 sailing ships totalling 52,634 tons, or about 77.5 per cent of its ships and 95.6 per cent of its tonnage. Then, when the war ended, as Andreas Lemos describes, the Greek shipowners sallied out with the impetuous courage of generations, and with the experience gained in years of struggle, and won the greatest prize in the history of the Greek Mercantile Marine, which might well be called 'the new Greek Miracle': a merchant fleet of 3,000 ships totalling 22 million gross register tons! All types of ships – super-tankers, bulk carriers and smaller vessels of all trades – came within the scope of the Greek shipowner's activities.

In 1982 the Greek-owned fleet had grown to 4,351 ships (50.6 million tons). In 1994 the Greek fleet of tankers, bulk carriers, container ships and the rest – more than 20 per cent of the merchant fleet of the world – is some 104 million deadweight tons.

John Hadjipateras rightly claims that in the 1990s the Greek shipping community who manage that huge tonnage are a force to be reckoned with – 'after all we are the major transporters of goods round the world'.

They have earned that pre-eminence in world conditions which, in so many respects, conspired to block any progress in the provision of swifter and cheaper sea transportation. As is pointed out by Pegasus Ocean Services Ltd – at the head of which was the vice-chairman of the Greek Shipping Co-operation Committee, Michael Peraticos – during the 1970s and early 1980s the industry learned some hard lessons. But the final decade of the century may be bringing with it a recovery phase with prospects of increased profitability. The quadrupling of bunker prices in 1973/4 was instrumental in defining a new phase in shipping. After a period of intense scrapping, fleet numbers were reduced, and the world's shipping fleet levelled out at the sensible and pragmatic tonnage sufficient to source available business.

As shipping transportation faces an upturn, however, so the world fleet is ageing. At the end of the decade 90 per cent of the world's supertanker fleet was more than ten years old, and 60 per cent was more than twelve years old. In 1994 output from the world's shipyards is at its lowest for twenty-five years, and personnel with shipping experience are diverting into other industries. Pegasus see charter rates earned by tanker owners as nowhere near presenting a feasible method of repaying the cost of a new ship. With new building prices continually escalating to keep up with construction costs, it is becoming increasingly necessary to prolong the life of existing shipping in order to maintain reasonable hire and freight costs. Although until recently it has not proved viable to run ships beyond a fifteen-year period on average, sophisticated modernisation programmes are beginning to have an effect on the market.

Pegasus Ocean Services is a typical Greek shipping agency in so far as it illustrates the devotion of Greek shipping families to the industry's complex details, in their case the Peraticos Xilas and Inglessis families who, before the formation of the group, had been in the shipping industry and operating ships

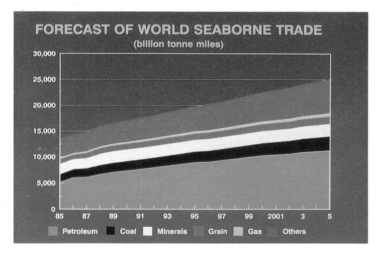

The ever-growing needs of the world are fed and fuelled by sea transport.

for more than a hundred years. They are less typical perhaps in that twenty-five years ago they decided to develop friendship into business advantage. In any other field than Greek shipping, says Pegasus in describing their own enterprise, co-operation would have appeared as a foregone conclusion, 'but the average Greek shipowner tends to be insular and individualistic'. In an industry so susceptible to all the whims of commerce – weather, politics, agriculture, labour and intense competition – they claim Pegasus represents a singular success. With their fleet's cargo-carrying capacity in the late 1980s and early 1990s of 1.5 million dwt, Pegasus was firmly in the league of the twenty largest Greek shipping groups, which include such names as Niarchos, Agelef, Seatrans and N J Goulandris.

The group's growth began with their purchase in 1964 of two 37,000-ton bulkers from Mitsui. Two years later they signed their first contract with Ishikawajima Harima Industries for a new 'Freedom' multi-purpose cargo vessel which gave them, as a world-wide cross-trading tramp operator, a new degree of flexibility. A further nineteen of these ships were ordered, and 'Pegasus became one of the largest operators of multi-purpose general cargo ships in the world'. They did their first big bank borrowing in the mid-1970s in order to raise the $18 million to buy two newly completed 18,000-dwt geared bulkers from a South Korean yard, and another $8.5 million for an 18-month-old Bulgarian bulker. They renewed their fleet with the new building of bulk carriers in Denmark, and were among the first to place an order for the Freedom Mark II. By 1980 they had taken delivery of another four 17,800 dwt Mark IIs. In 1984 Sunderland Shipbuilders built them bulk carriers suitable for the Great Lakes.

It was their final 'new building'. A large proportion of the world's tramp shipping vessels, as they point out, has not been built for any specific contract – it plies for hire all the time. Since 1970 they have been responsible for 1,700 charter-parties and have serviced all the needs of one hundred ships. Between 1990 and 1993 they bought and sold twenty-seven ships at a cost of more than $180 million.

Until the end of 1988 all four of their very large crude carriers were engaged on Iran's shuttle system linking Kharg Island with the southern Gulf. Before they sold her, their Panamax products tanker was for some years on charter to Shell International Petroleum; they are chartering four of their recently purchased multi-purpose vessels to liner services.

Their base is London, though they also have offices in Piraeus and New York.

> London remains the world's most important shipping centre. The brokers in the Group's Chartering Department attend the Baltic Exchange where much of the world's chartering business is concluded. In close co-operation with their colleagues in other offices, the Operations Department runs the ships on a day to day basis, instructing ships' masters and dealing with agents in practically every harbour in the world. (*Pegasus brochure*)

They have a conservative philosophy when it comes to finance. They make it a rule to place a healthy amount of equity capital into purchase, regardless of whether 90–100 per cent finance is available. They make sure that their debt is amply covered by the asset value. There is no typical Pegasus deal, however. The amount of credit they have accepted in the past has varied from 45 per cent up to a joint venture with a bank at 90 per cent. During

George Papoulias, Greek Ambassador to the United Kingdom in 1991 (second from right) with the chairman of the Greek Shipping Co-operation Committee, John Hadjipateras, in the Queen's Room at the presentation of a model of the Karteria to the Baltic Exchange. Chairman and vice-chairman Paul Vogt and Peter Tudball received the model, which remains on display on the Floor as a symbol of the key role of the Greek shipping community in Baltic affairs.

high interest periods in particular, prepayments have been a not uncommon feature of their financial behaviour, decreasing risk and ultimately increasing the return on investments.

> Wholly owned companies are able to develop successful democratic management. Decisions in Pegasus have traditionally been taken by committee consensus, without even a chairman. This 'blunt pyramid' system has worked extremely well, with few of the hesitations that such democracy can cause from time to time. One of the most interesting and significant features of the Group is that a young generation of the principals' families is playing its part both in London and Piraeus. These refreshing influences have been responsible for London's new and highly computerised offices. The Group is now making full use of currency hedges, swaps and other financial instruments, and the initiation and follow-up of new business is practised with zeal and commitment.

The Royal Bank of Scotland have estimated that the total Greek shipping community spread across the world have liquid funds of around $40 billion. Between 150 and 200 Greek shipping offices have representation on the

Baltic Exchange; two members of its committee are Greek. Membership of the Baltic, says John Hadjipateras, is the most important part of being in London. 'We could not do without it.'

The shipbrokers of the Baltic could not do without the London Greeks. The Greek miracle more than compensates them for the decline of the British merchant fleet. Cross-border business is done in London because London is a strong market, and it is the presence of the London Greeks that makes it strong. Any market needs business in its own home town; the London Greeks are the Baltic's backbone.

Many British owners, of the kind whose origins have been briefly told, made their entrance onto the world shipping scene as brokers, and retained that side of their business after abandoning ownership of the tramp ships from which they found themselves unable to make enough profit. Others, however, such as Harris & Dixon, have never had reason to divert from shipbroking as their main line of activity. Like so many others, they branched out into insurance and, with links going back to 1801, were once the oldest insurance brokers at Lloyd's. In 1968, by acquiring Guestair Ltd, formerly Abbott & Gerson Ltd, they extended their traditional broking activities into the air freight business.

But so far as the Baltic is concerned, Harris & Dixon are the institution's oldest shipbroking firm, claiming foundation in 1797, and they hold that their charter-party of 26 July 1813, for the voyage of the *Jaines* to and from Archangel, is the oldest one to exist on the Exchange. The charter-party is signed by John Ord and James Bentley. The latter in 1810 became a partner with his uncle Goland Burton, who in 1797 had opened an office in Wapping as the familiar combined coal factor, ship and insurance broker. In 1841 shipbrokers Burton & Bentley became Bentley, Harris & Dixon, and when James Bentley died in 1846 the firm adopted the name of Harris & Dixon which it still carries. It was James Dixon of 81 Gracechurch Street who, in 1899, lobbied the Baltic Committee to consider moving to a site in Fenchurch Street when the South Sea House lease ended.

The firm which since 1976 has been known as Anderson Hughes & Company on the merger of Anderson Green with Birt Potter & Hughes, two wholly owned subsidiaries of P & O Steam Navigation, also originated in 1797 – with shipbroker James Thomson starting business on his own account in Billiter Square. James Thomson & Company were given the London agency of the captured French vessel which Lieutenant Alexander Anderson RN had purchased in 1815 and was trading to the West Indies with himself as master.

In 1842 Thomson agreed to take the lieutenant's nephew, James Anderson, as a partner. Twenty years later James's nephew, J G Skelton Anderson, became a partner, whereupon in 1863 the company styled itself Anderson Thomson & Company, changed in 1869 to Anderson Anderson & Company. When this partnership dissolved in 1919 the business was amalgamated with F Green & Company as Anderson Green & Co. Ltd. Part of the combined business acquired by the new company was management of the Orient Steam Navigation Company (registered in 1878). One of their directors was Lord Inchcape. They acted as their own brokers for the trading to the West Indies, while Bevan & Tozer acted for Australia.

H Clarkson & Company, the company which, with forty-three brokers on the Baltic, is the largest corporate member of the Exchange, has grown from the business which 22-year-old Horace Clarkson started with Leon Benham

Harris & Dixon Ltd are London's oldest City broking house. The illustration shows their head office as it was around the time they began their undertaking, in 1876.

in 1852. Clarkson was admitted a member of the Baltic, raising the membership to 628, at the meeting of the Baltic Committee in South Sea House in July 1858, the first attended by the new secretary, William Oxley. It was the occasion on which they declined the offer of a telegraphic service from Julius Reuter which would have given them the times of arrivals at Liverpool and Southampton of American, Brazilian and West Indian steamers along with 'all interesting political and commercial news'. H O McCoy, the company's chairman in 1994, rightly claimed that Clarksons have grown to be one of the world's largest shipbroking groups, employing more than three hundred people. Two hundred of these are brokers and support staff in the UK, and another hundred are based overseas. Their service embraces every aspect of world shipping: tanker and gas chartering, dry cargo chartering, sale and purchase, new building contracting, bunker broking and ship's agency, and freight futures broking. A recent venture is Cruise Brokers Ltd, engaged in the sale, purchase and chartering of passenger vessels. A large research team compiles and interprets data on the world's bulk and offshore fleets of more than fifteen thousand vessels every day. They are publishers of the widely read *Shipping Intelligence Weekly* (among other publications).

The West Hartlepool Steam Navigation Company, still a member of the Baltic, which it joined in 1904, is an example of a shipping company which is no longer a shipowner but acts under the same name as chartering brokers – for Far Eastern clients. Founded in West Hartlepool in 1856, the company opened an office in London in 1904. Ninety years later it still has an office in London – in the Minories – and a representative of the West Hartlepool Steam Navigation Company, in its new role as broker, attends the Exchange on a daily basis. Head office is still in Hartlepool.

Eustace Erlebach, a second-generation German born in Wiltshire who became a member of the Baltic in 1886, was never a shipowner. As a youth of 16 he was engaged as an assistant in 1869 by Thomas Lawrence in his Eastcheap shipbroking office. Erlebach became a partner in T C Lawrence & Company in 1880 when the firm had built up a good business in the West Indies and Russia trade. Five years later they opened an office in Paris. Lawrence retired in 1886, and it was Erlebach & Company which moved the business to Billiter Street, handling the shipment of sugar from Germany to North America. Eustace's son Donald came into the firm in 1901 and six years later was made a partner. Donald Erlebach was elected a director of the Baltic in 1926, having joined in 1902. A mainstay of the business between the wars was Albert Edward Morris, who had joined the staff in 1921 and became a partner in 1946, at a time when Erlebach's were appointed London chartering agents for the United Africa Company.

Albert Edward Morris of Erlebach Shipbrokers. Elected to the Exchange in 1930, he was a director 1959–65.

Donald Erlebach's half-century membership of the Baltic was marked in 1953 by the presentation to him of an illuminated address. It was the first occasion on which a member had completed fifty years and been a director at the same time. He came over to St Mary Axe as a member of the London Shipping Exchange, which he had joined in March 1902. He served as a director for three periods: 1926–9, 1937–43 and 1946–52. For twenty-five years he was secretary of the Baltic Exchange Golfing Society, and then treasurer; and from 1926 he was treasurer of the Baltic Exchange Amateur Dramatic Society. He took his son John into partnership in 1953. The business was incorporated as Erlebach & Co. Ltd, shipbrokers and chartering agents, in 1959. In 1965 Lord Kilmarnock, chairman of the Baltic, and the directors made Donald Erlebach, who had by then achieved more than sixty years on the Exchange, an honorary member at a ceremony following a lunch in his honour.

In 1994 Erlebach Shipbrokers are still operating, but are wholly owned by Howe Robinson Shipbrokers Ltd. They concentrate on fixing sugar cargoes, many under an exclusive arrangement. Erlebach's are one of the leading sugar brokers in the world. The company's principals charter in both raw and white sugar, in bulk and bagged. Their exclusive client base includes C Czarnikow Sugar, Booker, Vitol Sugar based in Geneva, Paris-based Jean Lyon, and several Japanese trading houses.

Foster Howe began his partnership as broker and chartering agent with B T Robinson in 1883. Robinson was the son of the senior partner of shipowners Robinson & Rowland of Whitby. Howe Robinson & Company were appointed brokers for a number of Whitby-owned steamships. They opened an office in Bishopsgate, London, moving later to Bury Court and St Mary Axe. They built up connections with many owners in Cardiff, and by 1920 had severed connection with Whitby. In 1937 Howe Robinson were working all the Dene Shipping Company business; ten years later, with World War 2 behind them, they signed up Jardine Matheson as clients to and from the Far East. Good brokerage was provided by the Silver Line. In 1973 Howe Robinson and Jardine Matheson formed Mercator Chartering, a joint venture with Canadian Transport of Vancouver, the transport arm of forest products specialist MacMillan Bloedel. The Seabridge Consortium had been formed three years earlier and, thanks to the inclusion of the Silver Line, Howe Robinson became one of the accredited brokers – and then in 1972 Silver Line was sold. When the freight futures market opened in 1985 Howe Robinson formed, with Gerard & National, a joint company they called GNI Freight Futures.

Silver Line Ltd was registered as a public company on 24 November 1925 with Stanley Miller Thompson as founder chairman. It operated as a cargo liner company world-wide until 1951, when it became involved exclusively in tramp trades and the time-charter market. This change in trading pattern followed the acquisition of Silver Line by Dene Shipping Company in 1950 and the appointment as chairman of Henry Barraclough. In 1959 Henry was succeeded by his brother Willie, who headed the company until 1966. For a time after that Henry's son David Barraclough was chairman, and then, until 1974, chartering director Donald Bull took over as chairman. In that year Silver Line became part of the Boris Vlasov Group of Companies, with Robert Crawford as chairman and Renato DePaolis as managing director.

In 1994 the V Ships fleet under the direction of president Tullio Biggi consists of some two hundred owned and managed vessels operated from Vlasov Group offices in Monte Carlo, New York, Cyprus, Southampton and London. The hundred or so vessels under commercial management are controlled by Silver Line, whose managing director Tony Crawford is a frequent visitor to the Baltic Exchange. The latest addition to the Vlasov Group fleet is the specialised passenger cruise liner *Silver Cloud* owned and operated by Silversea Cruises. It was scheduled to arrive in the Thames on 4 June 1994 as part of the celebration of the fiftieth anniversary of the D-Day landings in Normandy.

Steady coal business in 1877 gave a start to the Baltic member company known in 1994 as Eggar Forrester. Alfred Cheney and Samuel Eggar secured the agency of both the Albion Steam Coal Company and the Trocdipheid Coal Company, which led to the chartering of ships to a variety of ports where coal was sold on c.i.f. terms (including cost, insurance and freight). Soon their activities had spread around the world, reaching the Philippines, Australia and South America. Their shipping of chalk from the Thames to New York continued until 1955; grain trading from Sydney to the UK began in 1905. When Graeme Forrester joined the firm in 1892 it became Cheney, Eggar & Forrester. William Parker, who became a partner in 1906, introduced ship management, in particular of the five steamships of the Westminster Shipping Company.

Trading was the company's main business, and in 1921 they opened an

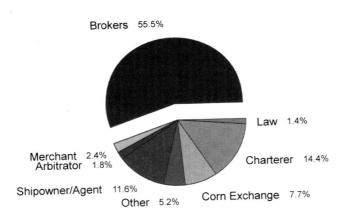

BALTIC MEMBERS MAIN COMPANIES BUSINESS

Brokers 55.5%

Law 1.4%

Merchant 2.4%
Arbitrator 1.8%

Charterer 14.4%

Shipowner/Agent 11.6%

Other 5.2%

Corn Exchange 7.7%

Other: Trade Assn, Equipment, Ports

Merchants, who dominated the Exchange before World War 2, have given way to charterers and brokers. Many of the brokers act for overseas shipowners, particularly the Greek shipping community.

office in Baghdad, shipping dates, barley and wheat from Iraq, while dominating the nitrate trade from Chile. In the 1930s as Eggar, Forrester & Verner they represented a Bombay company mostly in sugar chartering; in 1937 they were appointed chartering agents for the Seaboard Shipping Company of Vancouver. When Peter Talbot Willcox, chairman of Eggar Forrester in 1994, joined the firm in 1948 the Iraq business was still going strong. After six months of book-keeping, he remembers, 'Norman Eggar put his head round the door one day and announced that he wanted me to go, together with Haji Palmer, to Iraq. We were to help with the liaison work arising out of Eggar, Forrester's considerable purchases of barley from Murad Joory and dates packed by Salman Daniel.'

In the 1950s further connections were started with Bombay in the form of chartering business with Timblo Brothers; a branch was opened in New York; projects were launched with Japan; a tanker department and an S & P department were planned. Jock Ropner and Sir Guy Ropner joined the Eggar, Forrester board of directors, and Ropner's made a substantial investment in the company's shares – it was Ropner's who made the first move with tankers. When the company merged in 1960 with BOECC Ltd, Ropner's became 51 per cent shareholders in the new Eggar, Forrester & Verner Group of which Jock Ropner became chairman. In 1969 they formed the Wilks Shipping Company to manage the first of five 400 dwt coasters.

Percy Harley, whose company Harley & Company has become what in 1994 is Harley Mullion, began his career in shipping at the age of 17 when in 1881 he became a junior partner of shipbroker Craven & Company in Great St Helen Street, which earned him 10 shillings a week. Three years later he first entered South Sea House as an elected member of the Baltic. 'I have been on there ever since almost daily', he recollected in *My Life in Shipping 1881–1938*, 'but perhaps only about ten members who were members in 1884 still remain with us now [1938]'. He remembered William Oxley, the secretary, as 'a quiet amiable gentleman who sat at a small raised desk at one end of the Room always visible and accessible to the members'.

He disliked the little round tables at the end of the Room covered with white marble tops, 'the same one sees in the cheap Italian ice-cream shops', which he thought hideous and out of place in the Baltic of South Sea House – though in full keeping in an Italian shop. Brokers like him had to cultivate the Greek and British grain merchants who sat at those tables, and had opportunities of doing so 'quietly at a discreet distance, watch them partaking of their necessary but modest midday repast'. At what he judged the right moment he would:

> respectfully mount the two steps to my merchant's temporary throne and suggest respectfully that his immediate confirmation at the increased modest price of sixpence on that which, previous to lunch, he had stoutly refused to give, be now afforded so that lunch and fixture could end happily at the same time. On rare occasions it did, but on others, owing perhaps to a rapid setting in of indigestion it did not, or rather a reduction of a shilling was insisted on. (*My Life in Shipping*)

Percy Harley brought James Mullion into Harley & Company in April 1938. Mullion, who was of Irish-Scottish extraction, soon became a shareholder and a director. The firm was restyled Harley Mullion & Company and had offices in the Baltic Exchange building, which they occupied until they were bombed out in 1992. They specialise in S & P but also have a small business in tanker and dry cargo brokering. Roderick Mullion, James's son, is a director of the International Petroleum Exchange for hedging against changing bunker prices, and advises on finance and the petroleum futures market. His chartering clerk/representative pays the Baltic a visit regularly every week.

In 1994 Galbraith's Ltd are shipbrokers – with twenty-three brokers in Baltic membership. It was the shipbroker and commission agent business started by two Scots, William Lindsay and his brother-in-law Angus Stewart, in London in 1847, which set in motion the chain of events that led to the similar but greatly larger enterprise which a seventy-strong staff are conducting in Hay's Galleria off Tooley Street 147 years later.

Before their business was twenty years old, like many others, they had also become shipowners and become involved in insurance broking at Lloyd's. Shipowning became a major activity when in 1869 another Scot, James Galbraith, became senior partner of the firm, which had moved from Abchurch Lane to Austin Friars. With Glaswegian James Henderson, already a shipowner, they formed the Albion Line for the refrigerated cargo trade with New Zealand (sold to Shaw Savill in 1882). This led to James Galbraith creating the Irrawaddy Flotilla Company and the British & Burmese Steam Navigation Company which opened up inland trade with Burma and overseas. In 1877 Galbraith Pembroke & Company had the first ship for them on their own account. James Galbraith died in 1885 and thirteen years later his companies were grouped as Austin Friars Shipping Co. Ltd which continued trading until 1952 with the sale of their last vessel.

Galbraith Pembroke had never abandoned shipbroking, however, and it now became their main business. It was strengthened when, in 1968, the firm became part of the Matthews Wrightson Group, whose

Matthews Wrightson Burbidge Ltd had been shipbrokers and chartering agents since 1901. After three years as a member of the Samuel Montagu Group, in 1987 senior management and staff of Galbraith's Ltd acquired the subsidiary companies of Galbraith Montagu Holdings. With the backing of the Miller Insurance Group, who have a 23 per cent shareholding, Galbraith's Ltd serve the shipping industry through three major departments, dry cargo, tanker chartering and S & P.

When E A Gibson Shipbrokers Ltd celebrated their centenary with a banquet in London's ancient Guildhall in August 1993, it was an occasion for congratulating themselves on their good fortune to have been led through such a turbulent period of history by a succession of forceful characters, headed by their founder Edward Aisbett Gibson who took over all Hunting & Son's shipbroking in 1893. He was succeeded on his death in 1913 by his son Archibald. Bill Green, who joined as a 13-year-old office boy in 1916 and cornered the creosote market for Gibson's when a chartering clerk in his teens, as managing director gave the firm a reputation throughout Europe as the principal brokers for crude oil sales. He opened offices in Morocco and Calgary, and started an aviation department. Eric Shawyer, who joined the dry cargo chartering

The face of modern sea trading.

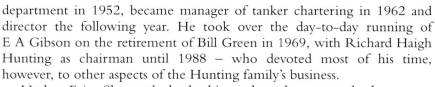

Eric Shawyer (right foreground), chairman of E A Gibson & Co. Ltd, still believes in hands-on broking and his desk is with his team in this typical hi-tech office.

department in 1952, became manager of tanker chartering in 1962 and director the following year. He took over the day-to-day running of E A Gibson on the retirement of Bill Green in 1969, with Richard Haigh Hunting as chairman until 1988 – who devoted most of his time, however, to other aspects of the Hunting family's business.

Under Eric Shawyer's leadership, other dry cargo brokers were acquired and an S & P department was formed. In 1973 E A Gibson Shipbrokers Ltd was created, and two years later the company re-entered dry cargo chartering under its own name. A gas chartering department was opened in 1980 and an offshore department in 1985. They claim to have achieved in a hundred years 'a happy blend of spread and specialisation' – and without ever being shipowners.

The Vogt family background was not in shipowning but in shipbuilding – and in Norway. In 1994, however, Vogt & Maguire serve shipping not by building ships but by owning them, chartering them, arranging for their sale and purchase, and being port and liner agents.

Johan Vogt came to England as a young man determined on a career in shipping of some kind. He left behind a father connected with the great Norwegian shipping yard at Moss, still known to the older generation as the Vogt Shipbuilding Yard. His first years in England were spent in Liverpool, Leith and Glasgow. From his meagre earnings of those days he saved several hundred pounds, which he pooled with a similar sum from James Maguire to form the partnership of Vogt & Maguire. That was in August 1895, and he was aged 28. They began by importing ice from Norway.

In 1897 Johan married a girl from a family who had been in shipping for many generations as captains of their own ships and as shipowners. Through his wife Jenny's connections, he gained entry into the whaling industry and began selling oil to Lever Brothers. Vogt & Maguire came to act for most of the whaling companies, serving particularly the mother ships which bunkered in South Wales for the season's fishing. By 1904 – which saw the arrival of Johan's son, also Johan – the company were busy chartering Canadian spruce and salt, with voyages to the Far East and S & P new building contracts and liner representation. Johan sent his son to a public school, Rugby, which Johan Junior left in 1923 and thereafter joined the family shipbroking firm.

> Completely green business-wise [wrote Johan Vogt Junior many years later] I was sent to the Cardiff office as office boy and started learning the business from the bottom up. Business was not good. Shipping firms had gone, and were going, bankrupt right, left and centre. Scandinavian banks were failing and profits difficult to come by. My experience in my early business career left me with a determination to follow my father's policy of thrifty business finance, but hopefully looking round for chances to develop.

He bought James Maguire out in 1920. Canadian spruce remained their main chartering interest but they tried other activities such as a

Pisces Pioneer, a T & J Harrison-managed ship operating in the Pacific carrying coal and other bulk cargoes.

sherry agency and a soap agency. They closed their South Wales office and concentrated on Merseyside, Preston and Garston. Johan Vogt Senior died at the age of 77 in 1944. Paul Vogt, who joined the business from school aged 18 in 1956, leads it in 1994, the third generation to head the family enterprise which, progressing (in spite of being bombed out of its St Mary Axe office in 1992) 'from quill pen to computer', will next year celebrate their centenary. Vogt & Maguire have been a member of the Baltic from the outset; Paul Vogt was chairman before Peter Tudball and both have daughters who now represent their family companies on the Exchange.

Importing and selling Polish coal was the initial business of John S Hamilton when he formed J S Hamilton Ltd in January 1937. Two years later the enterprise was joined by Tadeusz Olszowski, Poland's first private deep-sea shipowner, who resumed full-time commercial activity after a period of war service. In 1948 J S Hamilton Ltd restarted selling Polish coal to West Germany, Egypt and Argentina; and the following year they resumed selling sized house coal to Ireland, Britain and Morocco. When John Hamilton retired in 1952 the company became the property of the Olszowski family, who continued and expanded the shipbroking services which had been a feature from the start. In 1952 Tadeusz Olszowski introduced refrigerated cargo broking and developed new markets for Polish coal in Portugal, Brazil and Spain. In the years that followed they were delivering to Uruguay, Goa, the Canaries, Sierra Leone and the Congo. They boast not only of having sold coals to Newcastle but also to the Vatican many years before the arrival of a Polish pope.

J S Hamilton opened an office in Poland in 1989 to provide supervision services for import and export cargoes. A few years later they formed Academy Maritime Ltd of Gdynia, in partnership with Merchant Marine Academy, to provide Polish seafarers for foreign-flag seamen.

SEVEN

DO AS YOU WOULD
BE DONE BY

for all who practise the Baltic Code

Ship agents as well as ship brokers and owners have for a long time enjoyed the benefits of membership of the Baltic Exchange. Among the oldest of the clan are John Good & Sons of Hull, who cover most ports of the world except for Australia and some countries of South America.

It was in 1813 that the 11-year-old John Good left his home in Scarborough, headed for the harbour and boarded the 140-ton *British Volunteer* sailing ship. It was the start of a life-time's association with ships and shipping between the east coast of England and the ports of the Baltic Sea. That first voyage of what was to be seven years' apprenticeship took him to St Petersburg. Having gained a master's certificate, he spent twenty years sailing in vessels trading to the Baltic Sea, the White Sea (between Archangel and Lapland) and Mediterranean ports. He 'swallowed the anchor' in 1833 and moved with his wife to Hull, where he set up as a ship's chandler. He became the supplier not only of the local shipowners but for all the Dutch, Greek, Scandinavian and Finnish vessels trading into Hull. Soon he was taking shares in ships, and by 1853 he had established himself as a thoroughly successful merchant, with particularly good connections with Finland. When he retired in 1864 his business was carried on by his sons Joseph and Thomas as John Good & Sons. Inevitably the next step was into shipowning and, in conjunction with Francis and James Rickitt, the two of them established the firm of Good Brothers & Company, shipowners. Their father died in 1876.

John Good & Sons became agents for a number of Finnish shipowners trading to Hull, Newcastle and Middlesbrough who later combined as the Finland Steamship Company, and in 1994 are still operating as partners in Finanglia Ferries. Incorporated as a limited liability company in 1908, John Good & Sons Ltd developed substantial connections as coal exporters and became appreciable operators in the time-charter market. Liner agencies and warehousing followed, and in the 1950s they opened a London office. In 1959 they formed General Cargo Brokers (Mercia) Ltd to handle liner

Discharging grain from a modern bulk carrier. The scale of the operation is indicated by the caterpillar track vehicles operating in the holds.

145

trades between the port of Ipswich and ports in Europe and the Baltic Sea. They reckon that in 1994 they are one of the few nationally-based independent and privately owned agents remaining.

The time when, before joining forces with the London Shipping Exchange, the Baltic had twice as many merchants as shipbrokers is long past, but in 1994 just over 4½ per cent are mercantile members – that is the trading houses with cargo to carry and seeking a ship they can charter to carry it in – who are the *sine qua non* of the whole exercise. Some of them, like Louis Dreyfus Trading Ltd, Usborne PLC and Frank Fehr & Company, have been members for more than a century.

Louis Louis-Dreyfus was elected a member in 1890 and remained one for fifty years until his retirement in 1940. Charles Louis-Dreyfus was a member from 1919 to 1930. In 1929 Pierre and Jean Louis-Dreyfus were elected to the Exchange and both continued their membership for fifty-nine years until they retired in 1988 – and in 1994 they are enjoying their retirement in the best of health in their native Paris. Throughout this century the Louis Dreyfus Group have consistently ranked among the top grain trading houses in the world, and as a result have been charterers of considerable importance. For them the Baltic has always been the centre for their world-wide chartering operations. There they are able to fix ships to execute the wide range of commodity contracts they trade with clients round the world. Throughout their history Dreyfus have chartered every shape and size of dry cargo vessel, from the old four-masted sailing barques carrying 5,000 tons of grain to the UK from Argentina and Australia in the early part of the century, to the modern coasters, handy sizes, Panamaxes and Cape sizes of today. The group's involvement on the Baltic has been three-fold, as commodity traders, ship charterers and shipowners, and up to the 1970s they were among the several mercantile members whose

SS Carolina, owned from 1870 to 1872 by Good Brothers & Company. The ship was bought to carry mail to the Cape and later traded to the Mediterranean and on the north Atlantic.

representatives attended the Floor where every day the great proportion of UK imported cereals and cattle food was traded.

Bernard Perl, a post-war director of Louis Dreyfus & Co. Ltd, served on the board of the Baltic from 1947 to 1953, and was chairman of the Exchange from 1951 to 1953. In 1994 John Brady, chairman of Louis Dreyfus Trading Ltd, was in his second term as a director of the Baltic.

The group became shipowners when, in 1903, the Louis Dreyfus company in Paris bought the ship on which a fleet was built up gradually over the next thirty years. In the 1930s they acquired a small British company, Buries Markes Ltd, which after World War 2 became the group's shipowning arm in the UK and was elected a separate member of the Baltic in 1948. By the 1980s the Dreyfus fleet had grown to some two million tons deadweight of owned, managed and operated tonnage, most of them dry cargo vessels but including two liquefied natural gas carriers. Those of the fleet which flew the British flag were owned and managed by Buries Markes Ltd and Sagland Ltd. After the war the Paris office created several shipowning partnerships, pools and joint venture investments. They inaugurated specialised liner services and expanded, up-graded and modernised the whole fleet, which in 1994 consists of about 2.5 million tons, mostly modern bulk carriers.

The Louis Dreyfus Group, engaged in many activities other than those which link it to the Baltic Exchange – such as real estate – have their headquarters in Paris and are still owned 100 per cent by the Louis-Dreyfus family under the presidency of Gerard Louis-Dreyfus, a great-grandson of the founder.

Usborne PLC have a very much longer association with the Baltic. Corn merchant Thomas Usborne was not one of the group of Russia merchants, Turkey merchants, commercial brokers, tallow chandlers and soap makers who formed the committee of the Baltic Coffee House Subscription Room in Threadneedle Street in 1823, but he was certainly a subscriber when a few years later he started the grain trading business which is still operating in 1994.

Major Usborne of Usborne & Son was one of the three delegates appointed by the Baltic Committee in 1865 to meet representatives of the Baltic Company who had bought South Sea House in 1858, 'with a view to arrive at a clear definition of the position of the two parties' with regard to members' dissatisfaction with the standard of service and amenities in the Room. The two parties were in fact the same, and each had the same secretary. The Usborne family of Sevenoaks was a preference share holder, one of sixty-two – in 1874 the family held nine thousand. Thomas Usborne became a director of the Baltic Company in 1895. He died in 1898. Usborne & Son were among the grain merchants who created the London Corn Trade Association in 1878, the first of whose contract forms was for East Indian wheat, followed by forms for the Black Sea and America.

There are no Usbornes in the company in 1994. Since the turn of the century they have been managed by members of the Frame family – William Frame in the 1970s and after him his son David Frame, who moved the office out of London, like so many others, to Micheldever near Winchester in 1989, the year in which he was chairman of the Baltic Exchange.

As the successor to the tallow business of Henry Fehr & Company, which moved from Zurich to London in 1857, Baltic member Richard Fehr Trading represents one of the few remaining commodity firms owned by the family or even with a member of the family working for them. In 1994 Richard Fehr, representing the fourth generation of the Fehr family, trades on his own, while his father Basil Fehr – who was chairman of the Baltic 1975–7 – runs Frank Fehr & Company (now mainly an investment company in property and land), the firm founded by his father who was chairman of the Baltic 1937–8 – perhaps the only instance of a father and son both being chairman. Frank Fehr took a great interest in the Exchange's sporting activities, and founded its tennis section. Basil Fehr, among many other appointments, was chairman of the London Commodity Exchange in 1954 and of the London Oil & Tallow Trade Association in 1956. In 1979 he was awarded the CBE for his services to the City of London and to the Baltic, and in 1991 he was elected an honorary member of the Exchange.

The success of the family business stems from Frank Fehr's realisation that Britain, impoverished by World War 2, would need to increase her exports as soon as it was over. By VE-Day he already had an export department in place under the management of A T Hopkins, lately retired from West Africa merchants John Holt and well acquainted with the textile market. He was assisted by Frank's son-in-law George McCarthy of H T McCarthy, silk merchants. The firm were soon handling hardware and many other goods besides textiles. By the time the war ended Frank Fehr & Company was one of the largest of its kind in Britain.

Mrs Margaret Thatcher, MP (now Baroness Thatcher), then leader of the opposition, is introduced to members by chairman Basil Fehr from the rostrum in 1978.

When Frank Fehr died in 1948 he had served the company for sixty years. With the gradual decontrol of commodities, it entered on an era of even greater prosperity under the direction of his sons Basil and Keith Fehr and the experienced traders who headed the various commodity departments. Transport and packaging were changing rapidly. In conjunction with Colyer Watson in Australia and New Zealand, Frank Fehr & Company were the first to ship tallow in bulk instead of drums. Realising that trade would tend to be done more from country to country and not through London (except for finance), Basil and Keith Fehr opened an office in the USA, Fehr Bros Manufactures, Inc., New York, for the import of textiles and later of hardware and steel.

When in 1952 Keith Fehr died from the shrapnel wound he received in his head on D-Day Minus One, the partnership was dissolved and became a limited company. Offices were opened in Durban and Vancouver; a partnership was formed in Sydney, New South Wales; and tallow storage tanks were built in Durban, Drogheda, Brisbane and Liverpool. Richard Fehr joined in 1960 and became a director in 1971. The business was at its height in the late 1970s and early 1980s. One year it was no. 11 in *The Times* list of the top 1,000 companies in the UK. However, stated Basil Fehr in January 1994, 'due partly to the recession but mainly to defaults by supposed-to-be respectable companies, it is now much smaller. Such events have happened before with a family firm which has been at risk for 135 years.'

In the year the Baltic Committee was formed, 1823, James Richardson was taken by his father Daniel at the age of 4 from his home in Aughnacoy in County Tyrone to Canada. James's mother had died shortly before father and son left Ireland, and Daniel died a few years after they had set up their new home in Kingston, Ontario. James, who was brought up by his aunt, met most of the local farming community through his first business venture, a tailor's shop. In 1857 at the age of 38 he started another business buying corn from his erstwhile customers and selling it. He was soon Ontario's leading grain merchant. He was joined in what was by then a thriving enterprise by his two sons, George and Henry, in the 1870s.

In 1883 James Richardson & Sons arranged the first shipment of grain from Western Canada by way of the Great Lakes to Buffalo for delivery to Liverpool. James Richardson died in 1892, and it was under the leadership of his grandson and namesake, James A Richardson, that the company transformed themselves during the 1920s and 1930s into a widely diversified enterprise. In 1936 they opened an office in London, their first overseas. Their port of delivery was still Liverpool, where in October 1929 they landed their first shipment of wheat ever sent to England via the port of Churchill on Hudson Bay. James Richardson & Sons Overseas Ltd took over from Heatley & Co. Ltd (established in 1857) the merchandising of Canadian grain and grain products in the UK and Europe. Their own grain brokers, Whitson, Neilson & Francis Ltd, dealt principally in UK domestic wheat and barley, both physical and futures.

Whitsons were founder members of the London Grain Futures Market in 1929, although they always passed their trade through Geoffrey Coley and then Coley and Harper Ltd. In 1987 the company were bought by Coley and Harper Ltd and continued trading physical and futures until, sadly, the operation was wound up in 1989 by the new owners of Coley and Harper Ltd, thus bringing to an end a company that had enjoyed

Moray Firth Maltings have sited their plants (overleaf) within the finest barley growing areas in the United Kingdom. A large proportion of their produce is exported to brewing undertakings overseas.

links with the physical grain trade, grain futures and the Baltic, for generations.

Much of the barley which farmers grow in Britain is bought for processing into malt. Baltic mercantile member Moray Firth Maltings of Arbroath in Scotland, who reckon they are the second largest producer of malted barley in the UK, sell 57 per cent of their production to brewers and ship nearly half of that to beer makers all over the world. The remainder they sell to distillers, 19 per cent of which they export. Their malt, of which they produce a large number of types to suit the end product, is the essential ingredient of a great diversity of alcoholic drinks from the traditional pale ales of England to famous international Pilsener lagers, from classic Highland malt whisky to the sophisticated distillations of Japan.

In 1994, at the ports where shipments of grain and sugar, bauxite and iron ore are discharged, all the services which every type of modern cargo vessel requires – towage, salvage, anchor handling – are provided by companies such as Wijsmuller of Ijmuiden in Holland. Engaged in the hazardous business of salvage and ship delivery (their first line of activity), they value their membership of the Baltic, apart from the contacts they can make, because of its reputation for maintaining high ethical standards and fair dealing. But the Wijsmuller Group are also into ship management, and their own group fleet is managed according to the 'all-in-one-hand' motto of their ship management experts. Their British subsidiary Seaspan Manning and Technical Services Ltd of Greenhithe specialise in ship delivery and crewing. Their Dutch subsidiary Marman BV provide brokerage services in chartering, and in the sale and purchase of tugs, supply vessels, pontoons and other support ships.

For a body that owns and manages an entire port in the 1990s, of the kind scattered all round the coast of the British Isles, keeping up to date on every aspect of international shipping is a high priority. The municipally owned Port of Sunderland at the mouth of the River Wear on the north-east coast became a member of the Baltic Exchange in 1986, and their representative in 1994 is their sales and marketing manager N F Curle. 'For us', says Frank Major, the general manager and principal, 'the Baltic is a very convenient and central point to meet with our London and southern based customers.'

Shipbuilding was being undertaken in Sunderland in the seventeenth century. By 1834, according to Lloyd's Register, it had the most important shipyards in Britain, producing half the total number and tonnage of vessels the kingdom built. Development of the harbour began with the appointment in 1717 of the River Wear Commissioners, who built the first pier – on the south side of the harbour entrance – in 1726. Isambard Kingdom Brunel's North Dock was opened in 1837 and the South Docks in 1850. Other piers followed, culminating in 1934 with the deep-water tidal Corporation Quay. In 1972 the River Wear Commissioners, who had spent £1 million on improvements over the previous twenty years, handed over ownership and control of the Port of Sunderland to the Borough of Sunderland. It is now fully equipped to handle every kind of loading and discharging – break bulk cargo, project cargo, cut-out roll-on roll-off, unitised cargo, container freight and bulk liquid.

Wijsmuller at work salvaging a casualty of the Iran–Iraq war.

Apart from municipal ports such as Sunderland, there are 114 trust ports created by individual Acts of Parliament (on their way to being privatised) and several company ports owned by public or statutory companies. In 1983, under the Transport Act of 1981, the government brought into being a statutory corporation called Associated British Ports (ABP) to take control of nineteen of the thirty-one ports which had been run by the British Transport Docks Board, and before them the British Transport Commission. The other twelve were sold or transferred to other port authorities.

ABP have since acquired other ports, and in 1994 from their London office they control twenty-two of them. They are the country's largest single port operators, handling a quarter of the UK's sea-borne trade, though local managers are responsible for the day-to-day running of their

own ports. ABP is a wholly owned subsidiary of Associated British Ports Holdings PLC, quoted on the London Stock Exchange, whose chairman is Sir Keith Stuart. The corporation has been a member of the Baltic since its creation.

The MV Anja *discharging malting barley at Goole in 1990.*

Every time a ship put in to harbour, her master had to report his arrival to port officials and if – as so often happened – he had cause to make a protest about some incident that had occurred *en voyage*, he sought out a notary public, a man publicly authorised to draw up and attest contracts, to attest his written declaration giving the circumstances under which injuries had been made to his ship or cargo, or his crew had incurred liability. A firm of notaries public who undertook a considerable amount of business of this kind were Cheeswrights, whose offices for a hundred years up to 1940 were opposite the Custom House on the Thames to which ships putting in to the Port of London reported.

In 1994 Cheeswrights are part of the 2.3 per cent of the membership of the Baltic in the category 'Law' – and one of the 100 per cent compelled to leave their offices in the Exchange building because of the explosion of April 1992. They moved back to Philpot Lane, which had been their place of business on two other occasions in their 215-year history.

Their association with shipping and the Baltic Exchange dates from the eighteenth-century firm of Clark & Gilson who combined their notarial practice with ship and insurance broking. Before joining Lewis Gilson, Thomas Clark set up as a notary public on his own in 1779, which Cheeswrights take as their foundation date. Lewis Gilson and his son Lewis Gilson Junior added shipping agency to the services they could provide. Lewis Gilson Junior's nephew, Henry Cornfoot Cheeswright, joined them as a third partner at the beginning of Queen Victoria's reign. It was Henry and his son Frederick Cheeswright who had the office in St Dunstan's Hill opposite the Custom House. The oath which Frederick Cheeswright took on being sworn in bound him to conduct the services which he rendered to the shipping industry to the same high ethical standards as those of the Baltic Exchange.

> I, Frederick Cheeswright, do solemnly sincerely and truly declare and affirm that I will faithfully exercise the office of public notary, I will faithfully make contracts or instruments for or between any party or parties requiring the same and I will not add or diminish anything without the knowledge and consent of such party or parties that may alter the substance of the fact. I will not make or attest any act contract or instrument in which I shall know there is violence or fraud and in all things I will act uprightly and justly in the business of a public notary according to the best of my skill and ability.

In 1931 Cheeswrights (then Cheeswright & Casey) amalgamated with an even older firm, Duff, Watts & Company, which had been founded by a Scot, William Dunbar, in 1771. In the 1950s they practised as Cheeswright Murly & Company. In 1994 Cheeswrights are the largest firm of notaries public in the City of London. Since 1958 the senior partner has been Anthony Burgess to whom in 1992 the Greek government awarded a gold medal for services to Greek merchant shipping. Managing partner Nigel Ready is the editor of *Ship Registration*, which Lloyd's of London Press published in 1991.

Aerial view of Garston, Liverpool, where traditional cargoes, steel imports and container traffic are handled.

The common denominator for these ship-brokers, charterers, shipowners, ship agents, ship managers, air freight carriers and brokers, grain traders, lawyers, notaries, arbitrators, trade associations, equipment manufacturers, port owners and managers, is membership of the Baltic Exchange – and London.

London has always been a centre for the world's sea-borne and air-borne carrying trade, and the ambition of Peter Tudball, chairman of the Baltic from 1991 to 1994, is to capitalise on the reputation which the Exchange has established over 250 years. That reputation is currently acknowledged by all the world's shipping communities, and makes the British capital city, which is the seat of the Exchange, the nucleus of a world maritime centre and forum. The Exchange serves not only those engaged in shipbroking and chartering, but also all the other ancillary activities of the international sea-borne and air-borne carrying trade. It is thus uniquely placed to advise governments, international organisations and traders. Says Peter Tudball:

Phosphates being loaded into a bulk carrier at Christmas Island.

> If no business is being done in London, if no fixtures are being completed, then you don't need the maritime arbitrators, the lawyers, the commercial court activity. Lloyd's marine insurance market would decline; the P & I Clubs would be less strong. All of these are in London and feed off the fact that there are shipowners and ship charterers with cargo to be carried in London through the medium of the Baltic Exchange.

That was why London was the stage for the whole of the international shipping scene.

Richard Ottaway – the solicitor who is an expert on maritime law, was for nine years an officer in the Royal Navy, is the Conservative MP for Croydon South and the parliamentary adviser to the Baltic Exchange – backs the plan. 'The essential role of the Government', he told *Lloyd's List* in August 1993, 'is to ensure London remains the leading commercial and maritime centre of the world. The huge contributions made to our invisible exports by shipbrokers and the Baltic Exchange in particular, gives it every incentive to do so.'

At the centre of the plan is the creation of a British open register. Its main target would be the quality international shipowners who want to put their business through London but are not eligible to use the existing register. It would also enable some of the British-owned ships currently flying other flags to come back and register in the UK. Of the thirteen million deadweight tonnage owned by UK companies in 1994 only around 3.5 million are on the mainland register. A further 1.8 million dwt are registered in the Isle of Man and Channel Islands, with 4.2 million dwt under the British flag registered in Bermuda, Hong Kong, the Cayman Islands and other British dependent territories. The reluctance of British shipowners to register their ships in Britain is because of the cost of manpower, their obligation to employ a specified number of British officers, and what they regard as other 'irritations' from the British Department of Transport.

When Hong Kong reverts to the Republic of China in 1997, many of their shipowners might have to seek a different flag, and hopefully they will switch to London. For commercial reasons, the Eastern Europe fleets, who since the break-up of the Soviet Union had become more international in their trade, might also seek to sail under a more international flag than their own. A bank will only lend money for the purchase of a ship if it knows it can place a mortgage on the vessel. A non-Ukrainian bank cannot place a mortgage on a Ukrainian flag ship since the laws of Ukraine do not allow it. There is no question of a loan, therefore. So East Europeans, if they want to become more international, will have to flag their merchant ships to a country where the banks can secure a proper mortgage – such as Britain.

In 1994 a large number of Russian ships are being flagged out to Cyprus, which has 22 million deadweight tons of ships under the Cypriot flag, as opposed to 3.5 million in the UK under the British flag. The Cypriot banks can mortgage the vessel and will therefore lend money for its purchase – as will banks in Gibraltar, Malta and the Cayman Islands.

> If you had a British Open Register [says Peter Tudball] with the kudos of a British flag, some of those Eastern European shipowners might say they would like to be a British flag so long as they did not have to conform to regulations that said they could not use their own Russian or Bulgarian crew. The government could write what sanctions it liked into the regulations. I want the British Open Register to be a Flag of Excellence not a Flag of Convenience.

The standards and regulations laid down by Britain in her Merchant Shipping Acts, the last major one of which was passed in 1988, are sometimes seen as harking back to the political and social circumstances of a hundred years ago. Under the proposed plan overseas owners who choose to register under the new British flag will retain their own taxation status and will not be brought into UK taxation on their international earnings. Restrictions on the nationalities of officers will be relaxed, but not on the certificates for crews and the standards for ships. The British government's Department of Transport will be empowered to reject an application for entry in the British Open Register on the grounds that the ship is too old or the standard of the ship and/or its crew is unsatisfactory.

In 1993 the Baltic Exchange commissioned Jonathan Packer, a member who is also a maritime consultant, to research possible structures for the register and assess the benefits it would bring to the British economy. Its introduction, the Baltic argues, would not require primary legislation. It would be administered as a distinct part of the registry which already handles such matters – but probably a new 'Registrar's Section' would have to be formed to keep the register. If the registry's surveyor-general's organisation, which inspects ships, were to be privatised, it might be that the British Open Register would become the responsibility not of civil servants but of private employees.

In the meantime, however, it was a matter of consulting maritime lawyers, Lloyd's Register, the Salvage Association, the Chamber of Shipping and others, making representations to the Shipping Policy, Emergencies and Security Directorate of the Department of Transport and meeting with their officials to assess the likely strength of government ministers' reaction. The Exchange formally set out their ideas on how the proposed register would enhance London's maritime influence in a letter to the Secretary of State for Transport in December 1993.

The attractions of London to overseas shipowners using the new register were clear, it said. As an operating base it had the advantages of a convenient time zone, a wide range of services and cheap office accommodation. Maritime London, including the allied services of broking, the law, insurance, banking and finance, salvage, ship classification, ship management and so on, would be enhanced. 'What benefits would the Government see? The presence of representatives of foreign principals in London with authority to procure shipping and related services and spend money, is key. Our emphasis is therefore on bringing business and employment to London.'

Jonathan Packer calculated that four hundred to eight hundred ships of 20 to 40 million deadweight tons would join the register over, say, five years. By the year 2000 London's shipping services, excluding insurance, might benefit to the tune of £40 million to £135 million. Such figures reflected only a modest 5 per cent or so of market trading ships transferring. Registration fees of between £4 million and £8 million a year would accrue to the government who, because of a larger British registered fleet, would retain influence in the IMO, the European Union, UNCTAD and other international forums. The United Kingdom could once again take the lead on international standards. The strengthening of London's maritime infrastructure should lead to greater employment in the related fields as new business is attracted.

For some time seminars on such matters have been held in London by the International Association of Dry Cargo Shipowners (Intercargo). Founded in the early 1980s to do for the dry bulk sector of shipping what Intertanko had been doing for independent tanker owners for many years, in 1994 Intercargo is the only international association concerned solely with that sector, and it is based in London – Bruce Farthing, the association's consultant director, has his office in Blomfield Street, EC2. Though membership was originally largely from Greece with a few members from Scandinavia and Hong Kong (where Dr Frank Chao, its chairman in 1994, does his business), it now has 160 members from more than twenty-eight nations representing nearly seventy million tonnes of dry bulk shipping. Forty members are in London. It stands for the principle of the freedom of the seas, free enterprise and free competition.

It might be thought, says Intercargo, that with the collapse of the command economy system in so many countries, and the apparent embracing of free market principles by the developing world, freedom would be guaranteed. That, however, is unfortunately far from the case.

Dr Frank Chao, chairman of Intercargo and president of Wah Kwong Shipping.

> The GATT negotiations continue to struggle. [They were concluded at the end of 1993, although shipping was excluded.] Meanwhile the development of regional trading blocs – NAFTA, EC, ANDEAN, ASEAN and so on – all seeking to expand their scope, raises the real possibility of regions developing free trade principles internally, but setting up protectionist or other barriers externally. The European Community is conceived by some in this way. (Intercargo annual review, 1993)

A bulk carrier in dry dock.

The activities of the London-based Intercargo contribute in no small way to the image of Britain's capital as the international maritime centre. The ships of one nation carrying the products of another will inevitably give rise on occasion to misunderstanding, misinterpretation and confrontation. Most would agree that objective assessment of the rights and wrongs in such cases is best made in a place which is home ground for neither party. The reputation of the experienced members of the London Maritime Arbitrators Association (LMAA) for being fair, speedy and cost effective has drawn disputing couples to London since long before the days of steam. In recent times they have pioneered short-term arbitrations and in 1989, as requested by the Institute of Chartered Shipbrokers, they introduced a small claims procedure. In 1993 some were advocating the adoption of the American Alternative Dispute Resolution system (ADR) of which the most common forms are mediation and conciliation, with awards which are not binding. With the backing of the Institute of Chartered Shipbrokers the LMAA and ADR Net Ltd conducted a pilot plan for ADR in the maritime field.

As Baltic member John Maskell, a shipping solicitor, believes, two parties who enter into a contract do so in order to adhere to it rather than

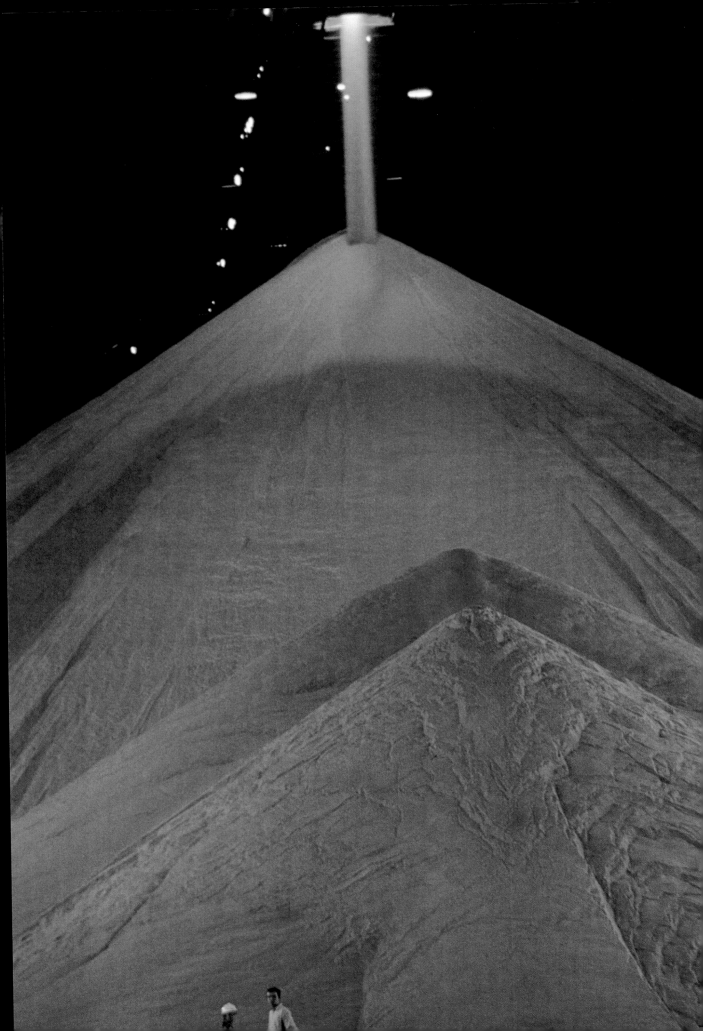

to use it as a prelude to legal action. A simple procedure should be available, however, in the event of unforeseen genuine disagreement.

> So often in fixture telexes one sees the phrase 'Arbitration London'. How many brokers really know what that means? Since the passing of the Contracts (Applicable Law) Act 1990 it is advisable, if a party wishes a dispute to be settled by a particular legal system, and in a particular way, to provide for that in the contractual document. Before the passing of the Act the phrase 'Arbitration London' would give the parties a single arbitrator who would hear the case in London and who would probably but not necessarily apply English law. It would have been open, if the parties were both foreign, to suggest that some other law be applied as the 'proper law of the contract'. As a matter of practice the arbitrator would work on the principle that English law and foreign law were the same unless he received evidence to the contrary, but it is not difficult to see that there is substantial scope for legal chicanery where one has provided for a place of arbitration but not chosen the system of law which is to be adopted. (*The Baltic*, April 1993)

An arbitration suite was built for the London Maritime Arbitrators Association in the Exchange building, and they moved into it on 1 April 1992. So they only had use of it for ten days before the IRA destroyed it – though not Arbitration London. Some 2,500 cases are referred to arbitration in London every year. About a third of these go forward to arbitrators, and the rest are settled before the parties meet. Much of the popularity of arbitration stems from its being held in private, a 'secret' meeting that is not reported, a feature that does not apply to the Commercial Court, which is open to the Press.

The cause of trouble is often negligence, and to guard brokers and others against their own, or another's, they make sure they are covered by 'errors and omissions' insurance for a genuine mistake. Indeed, the Baltic Exchange insist that every member holds such an insurance cover for a minimum of £100,000. The protection and indemnity clubs, through which they do this, were formed some 120 years ago when shipowners could not get *full* cover from Lloyd's, who at that time would only cover three-quarters of a hull policy. In the event of a total loss the owner had to pay for the other quarter. So shipowners got together and formed their own mutual clubs to cover that risk. In 1994, of course, the scheme covers a large area of claims other than the extra quarter – which Lloyd's do now provide for. If water gets into the hatches of a ship carrying a cargo of grain during a storm, and on opening the hatches it is clear that some 60 tons of wheat have been damaged, the shipowner would contact his protection and indemnity or P & I club, who would handle any compensation. If, while bunkering his ship, the oil spurted out and polluted the harbour, the owner would ask his P & I club to deal with the claim from the harbour authority. If a visitor to a ship tripped over a rope left on deck, broke his wrist and sued the shipowner, the P & I club would pay up. If a crate of wine landed on a stevedore's foot and broke it, his claim would be met by the P & I club.

Although in 1994 Lloyd's will now cover such claims, the mutual club system is what most shipowners subscribe to. They pay an initial 'call'

Bulk sugar inside the Queensland Sugar Corporation's storage sheds.

based on what the club estimates will be the amount they will have to pay out in claims that year. If, in the event, claims are higher than the estimate, members get an additional call. As a mutual club, it makes no profit but ensures it has ample reserves. The P & I financial year starts on 20 February because in the old days it was considered the first date when the ice would break in the Baltic Sea – 'First Open Water' (FOW).

In 1994 some twelve of the world's seventeen P & I clubs are in the UK. Forty per cent of the whole of the world's merchant fleet belongs to United Kingdom Mutual P & I Club, whose head office is in London. Others, such as the Newcastle P & I Club, of which Peter Tudball was chairman, are based outside London and have a much smaller number of members, though the eight hundred ships covered by the Newcastle club represent a cross-section of the whole shipping community – fishing vessels, tankers, refrigerated vessels, dry cargo and container ships and passenger ships. It serves about 3½ per cent of the world's merchant fleet.

When in 1925 a leading London shipbroking firm asked the Institute of Chartered Shipbrokers to help them recover a debt from a former principal, they were told that that was not part of the institute's function. As a result, several members created an unincorporated mutual association to serve members in this respect – the Chartered Shipbrokers Protection Association Ltd. In 1929 it extended its service to insuring members for claims for professional negligence, and changed its name to the Chartered Shipbrokers Protection and Indemnity Association. In 1970, with more and more shipbrokers and agents outside Britain applying to be similarly insured, the managers of the CSP&I formed the separate International Shipbrokers & Agents P & I Club which by 1982 had three hundred members from forty countries, many more than the UK club. The following year therefore the two organisations merged as Chartered & International Shipbrokers P & I Club Ltd. In 1990 this CISBA Club joined forces with yet another club, Transport Intermediaries Mutual Insurance Association Ltd, established in 1985 by Thomas Miller & Son (Bermuda). A final amalgamation of all these non-profit-making mutual clubs occurred in September 1992 when they put themselves under the single management of the 900-strong International Transport Inter-mediaries Club Ltd (ITIC). The presence of ITIC adds another incentive for shipowners to look to London for what they need in order to conduct their businesses safely, profitably and with the stability that will enable them to ride the financial storms and social upheavals that history tells them the world is seldom without.

But the main reason for their coming to London is that they know that their business will be done there in an ambience of commercial integrity where straightforward dealing is the done thing and ostracism awaits the clever Dick who makes the commercial (and social) blunder of thinking he knows better. Many who come from abroad say they do their business in London because it is the only place where they can trust people. 'You cannot put a value on that', says the chairman of the Baltic.

> If there was no longer a market in London; if people decided there was
> no further need for the Baltic Exchange, you would get tremendous
> difficulties with shipping contracts. You would get delays, interference

from lawyers, from people who don't understand you have to do business quickly – though not of course taking advantage of the other party's ignorance and trading on it. If you have a ship ready today and you haven't got a cargo, every moment they waste will cost them money. You have to have a system that enables you to do business quickly without referring to lots of documents, forms and papers, without wrangling and arguments. This is possible on The Baltic because people know each other, and they know the extent to which they can trust the other man's word. If you know the person you are dealing with, you know how far you can go with him and trust him. The code is totally understood. No one would like it to be known that they had been suspended from the Baltic Exchange for breaking that code. (Peter Tudball)

In the spring of 1993 eight member companies who had been long overdue in paying their bills, or had breached the code in some other way,

The membership team – Jackie Harrison and Sarah Prentice with Hugh Renwick, membership adviser to the Exchange 1992–4 and previously a director.

Overleaf: GEM Europoort Terminal, one of the terminals of European Bulk Services, seen from the air.

had their names posted on the notice board on the Floor. Within a couple of days six of them did what they had been asked to do for the last three months. The shipowner who told a broker on the phone he was no longer dealing with him because he had been 'posted' on the Baltic Exchange, notwithstanding the fact that it was for a comparatively minor offence, was doing what in London was routine. Some think, however, that Baltic directors are not strict enough in enforcing the code, and do not possess strong enough powers, or maybe lack the will – thinking 'We mustn't rock the boat.' They see discipline, alongside declining business ethics generally in the City, as too lax. For them, control is not as firm as it used to be, and members' business suffers. 'When I first came on The Baltic', says Frank Cordell of Galbraith's, 'you were in fear of the Secretary and what he could do.'

Apart from investigating and penalising members who have breached the code, the board of the Exchange take all the usual precautions, as they have always done, to make it as certain as possible that no one is admitted who from their known past history might offend. Since April 1992 advising on the induction of new members and checking their credentials has been in the hands of Hugh Renwick, one-time Baltic director, for forty years a member as a shipbroker with Buries Markes and retiring as managing director of Nedlloyd Shipbrokers in 1991 following the transfer of the business to J E Hyde. As membership adviser to the chief executive, he interviews every prospective new member along with Jim Buckley, and they both impress on applicants the value of being a member of the Exchange in relation to the cost of it – in 1994 a one-off company entrance fee specially reduced to £500 for the 250th anniversary from the usual £2,000 and an annual subscription for an individual principal of £496 plus VAT. He indicates the security that comes from members of the same club dealing with one another, volunteering to conduct their business within the same framework, being

subject to the same restrictions and subscribing to the same ethical approach.

The latter was embodied in the Blue Book, and since January 1989 in the Yellow Book, *The Baltic Code, a Guide for Dry Cargo Brokers*. Under the heading 'Ethics', the book reminds members, and informs prospective members, that the motto of the Exchange, 'Our Word Our Bond' symbolises the importance of ethics in trading: 'Members need to rely on each other and, in turn, on their principals for many contracts verbally expressed and only subsequently confirmed in writing. The broad basis for ethical trading has long been regarded by The Baltic Exchange trading community as the principle of treating others as one would wish to be treated oneself.'

Practices which the directors consider do not accord with Baltic ethics include the offering by an organisation operating as a freight contractor or speculator of named tonnage against tenders without the authority of the owners or disponent owners; agents and brokers implying by Telex messages or otherwise that they hold a ship or cargo firm when they do not, in order to secure a counter-offer from a principal; off-setting against hire sums representing unspecified or vague claims; and withholding payment of commissions when due in respect of hire or freight earned and paid. They frown on the use of information obtained through members in order to effect business direct with overseas principals or their local brokers, thus by-passing the Exchange. They also regard as unethical the passing of information to overseas brokers or their agents in order to effect business direct with members' principals or with their overseas agents and brokers.

Before a broker quotes business on the Exchange from a source whose *bona fides* is unknown, he is expected to make reasonable investigations and communicate the result of them to anyone considering entering into negotiations. If he has not made or completed such checks, he should clearly make that plain to the other principal or his broker. 'Negotiating needs to be conducted with care and attention to detail, as there has to be complete agreement between the two principals for an enforceable contract to come into being ... Verbal communications outside chartering negotiations upon which a broker has to act should be re-confirmed back to the instructing company.'

Reopened in April 1993. Baltic Exchange Chambers once again proudly flies its Baltic flags.

Generally the parties to a charter-party have freedom to contract on such terms as they may agree upon. But the aim should be clarity of expression and the avoidance of ambiguity and inconsistency in clauses. If disputes arise which eventually come before the Commercial Court in London for decision, the judgement will probably reflect the presumed intent of the parties. Such a judgement joins the body of 'case law', the so-called Common Law not written down as an Act of Parliament, which develops therefore according to the changing needs of commerce. It is possible to contract out of Common Law, but not out of Statute Law enacted by Parliament. Certain aspects of Common Law, however, have from time to time been codified into Acts of Parliament such as the Merchant Shipping Act and the Marine Insurance Act.

Negotiations intended to lead to the conclusion, as a 'fixture', are conducted on the basis of 'firm offer' and 'firm counter-offer'. A firm offer is limited as to time and is definite as to terms. If it is accepted by the party to whom it is made within the prescribed period it becomes an enforceable contract. The signing of the formal charter-party that follows is the written confirmation and record of a contract concluded orally.

> It is a Baltic practice that firm offers may not be withdrawn before the expiry of the time limit except by agreement of the offeree. If a firm offer is unacceptable and a firm counter-offer is made, the effect of this is to reject the first firm offer, which is therefore no longer available.

The rate of commission is fairly well established in each of the tramp chartering markets, and the Baltic board view with disfavour attempts to gain a business advantage on the Floor by offering to undercut the usual rate. Should there be a dispute under a charter-party and the parties cannot find a solution, Baltic directors regard it as customary for the matter to be referred to arbitration in accordance with a charter-party clause.

> In appointing an arbitrator, a party is choosing a judge who, together with his co-arbitrator(s), will decide the matter objectively to the best of his ability on the documents and submissions made by each of the parties or, if a formal Hearing is required, submissions may be made then by the parties themselves or through advocates, e.g. solicitors and perhaps counsel. The tribunal's Award is final as to the facts, also as to law, unless appealed (under the very restrictive conditions of the Arbitration Act 1979) to the Court.

To the guidelines of *The Baltic Code* are added the rules of the Baltic Exchange. Last overhauled in 1976, they have not been substantially amended other than for subscriptions since 1984. However, ten years on with the emphasis on increasing membership, the chief executive is examining ways of broadening the categories eligible to join the Exchange, without diluting its central role.

> All members or individuals having the right of entree to the Exchange shall conform to and be bound by the Rules, for the time being, of the Exchange and shall as and when required by the Directors sign a declaration to this effect in such form as the Directors may specify. (Rule 26)

The rules deal, as have they always done, with all matters concerning the conduct of the Exchange – eligibility for election, fees and subscriptions, disqualification, detrimental and unbecoming conduct, notification of expulsion, suspension or censure and so on. Rule 32 states that any member who fails to comply with an arbitration award made against him will have his conduct considered by the directors, who shall have the power to deal with him as they think fit. Rule 37 states that no member shall communicate to the press or public the contents of any notice exhibited on an Exchange notice board. Under Rule 38 the directors have the power to forbid or prevent entrance to, or continuance in, the Exchange of any individual 'if it is considered in the interest of Members to do so'. These rules applied equally to the right of entry to the Queen's Room when it was reopened in April 1993, just a year after the bomb outrage, as the Baltic's Floor.

Deciding what sort of building members who kept to the rules and abided by the guidelines would enter, and where it would be, once the temporary occupation of the partially restored St Mary Axe premises ended, was top priority for the chief executive and directors throughout the following months. After a major review of the options, in October 1993 the chairman, Peter Tudball, addressed a letter to the Exchange's shareholders headed 'Meeting the Challenge'. It represented a radical shift in direction to ensure that the Exchange was strengthened and flourished.

> The move back to Baltic Exchange Chambers and the Queen's Room in April has left us using old fashioned premises which are inflexible and expensive with limited club facilities which are not ideal. Sadly, our historic building is not suited to today's business needs. We have an operating deficit of some £1 million annually, before investment income. Reliance on subsidies for membership activities from office rentals is no longer possible. Reduced membership, declining Floor attendance and inadequate club use all concern us and combine to produce a financial position which cannot be sustained in the longer term.
>
> Directors therefore believe a fresh start, in new accommodation, which retains the key focus of a Floor appropriate to our needs, is required.
>
> In the light of detailed assessments made by our professional advisers and after examining a range of options, the Board's view is that a restoration and reoccupation by the Exchange of the listed building would not be in shareholders' interests. It would use the bulk of your capital without any likelihood of a realistic return from property rentals. Moreover, because the building is subject to constraints imposed by the Grade II★ listing by English Heritage, the core parts cannot readily be adapted to modern use. We have not been able to identify a new business use, nor have we found other Exchanges or bodies who might use the historic areas. The solution lies in a large scale redevelopment of the whole site requiring massive capital. This is beyond our resources and inappropriate to our objectives, since it would expose us to the vagaries of the property market. The Board feels that redevelopment is for those who have the necessary capital and who are willing and able to carry the corresponding risks. The responsibilities and constraints applied by English Heritage will pass to whoever takes on the site, leaving the investment capital which we have at present available to generate income to support the Exchange.
>
> After very full consideration we have therefore developed a new strategy. Realising the capital value locked up in the freehold of the St Mary Axe site, whilst preserving existing reserves, is a major element of that strategy. At the same time, the benefits of membership need to be promoted at home and abroad, professional and club services improved and costs reduced.

The Board has therefore concluded that it should:

- Invite offers, which might include a joint venture, for our site, recognising that completion of a sale could take some time;
- Acquire a more modern and efficient building in the City, providing a Floor similar in size to the one in the Queen's Room, as well as better club facilities;
- Promote membership and the Exchange's regulatory role internationally;
- Encourage related bodies to join us.

Being a member of the Baltic community is what matters, as it has been for 250 years – being known as someone who has willingly adopted its code of conduct, which will endure no matter where the community gathers, be it at the Virginia and Baltic Coffee House in Threadneedle Street, South Sea House, St Mary Axe or who knows where?

By the time Alan Harper, who comes from the commodity section, had succeeded Peter Tudball, whose last duties included presiding over the banquet held on 24 May 1994 in the historic surroundings of the National Maritime Museum at Greenwich in the presence of HRH The Duke of Edinburgh, the Exchange's most senior honorary member, to celebrate the anniversary of the opening of the commercial resort and subscription room on that date in 1744 – the strategy had become an actuality.

So, far from ending with that celebration, the story of the Baltic takes a new turn. For some time the directors had been aware that the magnificent palace of Forwood and Bridges, which was right for 1902, was wrong for 1992. In 1994 that wrong has been righted.

APPENDIX

CHAIRMEN OF THE BALTIC EXCHANGE

1900–1994

1900–13	W Bridges Webb	1959–61	F P Whithouse
1913–16	H W Barnett	1961–3	Cyril W Warwick
1916–19	F N Garrard	1963–5	Sir Leslie W Phillips CBE
1919–22	C W Howard	1965–7	The Lord Kilmarnock MBE
1922–4	Newton Dunn	1967–9	W Amedee Fairclough
1924–8	Sir Ernest W Glover Bt	1969–71	Brian F Turner
1928–31	John E Parry	1971–3	A H D Granger
1931–3	Sir F Vernon Thomson KBE	1973–5	M T Turnbull
1933–5	Sir Herbert T Robson KBE	1975–7	B H F Fehr CBE
1935–7	Sir John Niven	1977–9	G R Newman
1937–9	Frank E Fehr CBE	1979–81	D R Donaldson CBE, MVO, AFC
1939–46	Sir Frank S Alexander Bt	1981–3	P L Harding
1946–8	Sir W Norman Vernon Bt	1983–5	H L C Greig CVO, CBE
1948–51	Sir Henry C Brewer MBE	1985–7	R B Hunt
1951–3	B H Perl MC	1987–9	D W Frame
1953–5	Sir J Gibson Graham MC	1989–91	P J Vogt
1955–7	R Tadman	1991–4	P C Tudball CBE
1957–9	R D Hyde		

W Bridges Webb *1900–13*

H W Barnett *1913–16*

F N Garrard *1916–19*

C W Howard *1919–22*

Newton Dunn *1922–4*

Sir Ernest W Glover Bt *1924–8*

John E Parry *1928–31*

Sir F Vernon Thomson KBE *1931–3*

Sir Herbert T Robson KBE *1933–5*

Sir John Niven *1935–7*

Frank E Fehr CBE *1937–9*

Sir Frank S Alexander Bt *1939–46*

Sir W Norman Vernon Bt *1946–8*

Sir Henry C Brewer MBE *1948–51*

B H Perl MC *1951–3*

Sir J Gibson Graham MC *1953–5*

R Tadman *1955–7*

R D Hyde *1957–9*

F P Whithouse *1959–61*

Cyril W Warwick *1961–3*

Sir Leslie W Phillips CBE *1963–5*

The Lord Kilmarnock MBE *1965–7*

W Amedee Fairclough *1967–9*

Brian F Turner *1969–71*

A H D Granger *1971–3*

M T Turnbull *1973–5*

B H F Fehr CBE *1975–7*

G R Newman *1977–9*

D R Donaldson CBE, MVO, AFC *1979–81*

P L Harding *1981–3*

H L C Greig CVO, CBE *1983–5*

R B Hunt *1985–7*

D W Frame *1987–9*

P J Vogt *1989–91*

P C Tudball CBE *1991–4*

BIBLIOGRAPHY

Hugh Barty-King, *The Baltic Exchange*, the history of a unique market (Hutchinson Benham 1977)

Penelope Hunting (ed.), *The Hunting History*, Hunting PLC since 1874 (1991)

Anne and Russell Long, *A Shipping Venture*, Turnbull, Scott & Company 1872–1972 (Hutchinson Benham 1974)

Andreas G Lemos, *The Greeks at Sea* (Cassell 1976)

Pegasus Ocean Services, 1993 brochure

David Burrell, *Furness Withy 1891–1991* (The World Ship Society 1991)

E A Gibson, *A Century of Achievement 1893–1993* (Seatrade Organisation 1993)

Hurford Janes, *Full Ahead*, the story of Brown Jenkinson & Co. Ltd, 1860–1960 (Harley Publishing)

John Sutcliffe & Son, *A History of the Company 1862–1987*

H Clarkson & Co. Ltd, *Serving the World of Shipping* (1993)

J S Hamilton Ltd, *Our Story* (1937–93)

Vogt & Maguire Group, *Worlds Ahead in Shipping and Transportation* (1993)

Johan Vogt Junior, *Memoir* (MS in possession of Paul Vogt)

John Good & Sons Group, *Shipping Transport and Integrated Services* (1993)

The History of Galbraith's (1993)

A Brief History of Eggar Forrester 1877–1977

Craig J M Carter, *Stephenson Clarke Shipping* (The World Ship Society 1981)

Peter Cox, *A Link with Tradition*, the story of Stephenson Clarke Shipping Ltd 1730–1980

Edward F Stevens, *A Record of the History of Houlder Brothers & Co. Ltd 1849–1950*

Anderson Hughes & Company, *Profile and History* (MS)

A E Jeffery, *The History of Scruttons* (1967)

Percy Harley, *My Life in Shipping* 1881–1938 (privately printed)

Philip Paul, *City Voyage*, the story of Erlebach & Co. Ltd 1867–1967 (Harley Publishing)

Nigel Watson, *The Bibby Line* (1807–1990) (James & James 1990)

Leonard Gray, *The Ropner Fleet 1874–1974* (The World Ship Society 1975)

H S Appleyard, *The Constantine Group* (The World Ship Society 1983)

Associated Bulk Carriers, 1967 brochure

P & O Worldwide (April 1993)

John Brady, *The Louis Dreyfus Group* (MS)

James Richardson & Sons Ltd, *JR, a Brief History*

Moray Firth Maltings, *Making the Finest Malt*

Wijsmuller Profile, *Out of This (Maritime) World* (1993)

Port of Sunderland, *Big Enough to Cope, Small Enough to Care* (1993)

The River Wear Commissioners, 250th anniversary souvenir (1968)

Associated British Ports, *Background Information Paper* (1993)

Cheeswrights, *Notaries Public in London for over 200 Years* (1993)

Intercargo, *Annual Review 1993*

J A Findlay, *The Baltic Exchange* (London, 1927)

INDEX

THE BALTIC EXCHANGE · LONDON *The "Floor" of the Exchange*